Alternative Facts

DEMOCRATS V. REPUBLICANS

RUSSELL C. ARSLAN

Table of Contents

Forward - Alternative Facts.

The present political climate is the most contentious in recent memory. It is not nearly as rancorous or personalized as was the case in the early 1800s, 1801 to 1809, when Thomas Jefferson was president. There is not nearly as much animus as the Civil War era, 1861 to 1865, during Abraham Lincoln's presidency. But, for most present-day Americans, it is the worst of times. Today's political arena is almost a Skins vs. Shirts mentality. Anger and hatred are pervasive and permeate the political landscape. What are the causes of the animosity between the right and the left? Why are politics so ugly? Why does it seem everything is based on falsehoods when we have a society with so many facts at its disposal? These questions are of great importance. The questions are simple but almost impossible to solve! Why we have personalized politics to a state of total partisanship is beyond me. The Rodney King phrase, "Why can't we all get along?" is apt.

There is a lot of conjecture on whether the right or the left properly represents our needs as citizens. All I know is they are at odds and very vocal. There are a lot of false positions relative to these competing political ideas. Stephen Colbert coined a word for alternative facts or false propositions that are being used instead of the truth. In 2005, he used the word "truthiness" when referring to lies. In an interview with Charlie Rose on December 8, 2006, Colbert sarcastically lamented, "Untruthiness is what I say is right. Nothing anyone else says could possibly be true. Passion and emotion certainly rule over

information." Truthiness is the belief or
assertion that a statement is based on intuition
and has the same validity as facts. For many
Americans, a statement without regard to
evidence, logic, or intellectual examination
has the same weight as a statement that is
factual.

The constant lies. The ever-greater
number of people who have made creating
false news a business coupled with hatred and
apathy have brought America to a crisis. If
you pull yourself back from the present-day
political hysteria and try to be objective, it is
impossible to view Donald Trump as anything
other than a person of the lowest ethical
standards. How can you respect a president
who doesn't respect the presidency? He is ill-
equipped. His moral compass points south. He
exemplifies the ugliness of American politics.
No other president in recent American history
has uttered so many lies and political
invectives. You may or may not have his
political values.

That is fine. Hopefully you don't have
his personal values. It is perfectly okay to be
either conservative or progressive. That is
your choice and your choice alone. Both sides
of the political equation have compelling
arguments. But, there is always a but. Trump's
tactics to gain political leverage is aberrant
and unacceptable. The mean-spiritedness of
his lies and the depth of his hypocrisy are
unpresidential at best. At worst, they might be
impeachable offenses. His values are born
from the malignancies of moral corruption. If
you tie your political wagon to him as a means
of obtaining your political objectives, you will
be disappointed.

Trump is not a populist. He is not the champion of the middle nor the poor. That is okay! What is not okay is that millions of people have bought into his lies and political diatribe to ease the pain of their existence. Millions of his followers are looking for answers to the question of why their lives are not meeting their dreams. The harsh realities of urban life have now entered rural America. White people are now facing what minorities in the cities have been plagued with for decades. The drug or opioid addiction problem in middle America is a new phenomenon. Crime and blight, once only problems in the big cities, are now pervasive throughout middle America. There is massive unemployment and a lack of opportunities in our once secure rural areas. The changes are hurtful and threatening to the very fabric of our traditional American core. People are looking for answers. They believe Donald Trump can bring back prosperity. The problem is, his political bent will not help the average American. I am not saying there is no place for conservative philosophy or the Republican Party. Both are important. However, you must understand who they benefit - it is the wealthy not the middle or poor. That is reasonable and a legitimate political position. But it does not solve the problems of rural America. It is important to endorse someone who will protect you concerns. It is also important not to let your desire for a political result pervert your integrity and diminish your values. Accepting the Republican philosophy and pushing for change is acceptable. It is honorable! Yet, it might not suit the needs of the middle classes or Middle America.

The contentious nature of our politics

of today is not normal. We have not seen this much acrimony in more than 100 years. The discord of today is certainly milder than the great divides that Jefferson and Lincoln faced. In a world that is more complex and sophisticated with greater amounts of knowledge, political acrimony can only cause great social damage. The premise of my book will be looking at the political philosophy of both parties and advocating for greater truth. The old mantra of conservatives who favored rugged individualism, limited government interference and marketplace determinations do not hold today. Progressives who hold to a social calling or the service of helping others are out of sync as well. The complexities of our urban life, relative to the rural values of yesteryear, makes seeking information all that more important. We are living by paradigms that no longer hold. It is my contention the more factual we are in viewing political issues the better decisions we can make. Truth, not alternative facts, must be the order of the day. When someone claims something is false news, if it really is, we should reject it. If it is the truth, describing it as false news is no more than pernicious lies that harm the very fabric of society. Do not buy into false news or truthiness because you are too lazy or too closed minded to seek the truth. You have to ferret out the facts when you are making political or social decisions. The only thing that cannot hurt you is truth. The truth might be hard to live with. The truth might diminish your standing with yourself or others. But, to deal from any other position makes you deal from weakness. Veracity should be the basis for all decisions. Follow the road that will give you some guideposts to seek the right path towards truth. Any analysis must be based on facts or certainty. We will set down some assumptions on what the political philosophies of the left and the right are based upon. We will seek truth and present corroborating examples of each political position. We need a psychological framework as well to present the disposition of both conservatives and progressives. Even with the truth in front of us, there are differences in how it will be interpreted. We will try to debunk alternative facts emanating from both sides of the political spectrum. We will speak the truth without favor or fear. Hopefully, when you view our approach to the truth and alternative facts you will see things more clearly. I am not asking you to view reality as I do. I just want you to see things through a different lens. Truth brings objectivity. Being impartial or pushing aside bias equates with the ability to have free will and recognition of other people's opinions. Our main problem today is we do not listen to competing ideas. We know it all. We cut off discourse and compromise. Knowledge, predicated upon real facts, clears the path to freedom. The notion of one's faith and the denigration of the truth of science are old doctrines that are still highly coveted today by the right. They limit, not expand, our existence. It is unfortunate but the old ways, not accepting science, still hold sway in today's complex and sophisticated world. We need truth to base our social and political constructs upon not old unwarranted beliefs and faith in the unknown.

Russell C. Arslan

Forward Alternative Facts #2

Let's push forward one final time with a discussion on alternative facts and their effects upon our political thinking. I want to anecdotally present what I call the American dilemma. We all pretty much use the same sources to get information. They are not that varied as people think. They are easily accessible. Many of us use traditional media sources such as NBC, CBS, ABC, FOX, CNN, MSNBC and the BBC. A growing number of people us read popular political blogs. A few important ones, like the Huffington Post, Drudge Report, Politico, The Hill, Slate, InfoWars and Salon are widely read. There are some more radical or reactionary sites like Breithbart, Instapundit, and The Blaze. There is a myriad of informational sources. Even with all this information at our fingertips we rarely have the same interpretation on events or philosophies.

Let me explain this phenomenon by describing a social outing with some of my friends. One of my good friends wanted to share his newly acquired second-home with the group of us who grew up together. We all share a common background. All of us are middle-class and came from the same middle-class neighborhood. We all went to the same high school. We even went to college together. But, there was a greater bond - we are all ethnic Armenians. We call ourselves cousins. Fortune has it that we all are relatively successful. We have known each other for more than 50 years. Our families are close. We have seen our children grow and have children of their own. Us cousins have been together all of our adult lives. On this lucky occasion a group of us met at my cousin's lovely home on Balboa Island near Newport Beach in Southern California. Like I said earlier, it was an occasion to have fun and catch up. We wanted to share our fortunate circumstances in life with each other. We wanted to reminisce about the past. It was a given that politics would come up. I promised myself I would be mute. I would keep my mouth shut. As usual, I would just take it because my political position had been one of the outcasts for many years.

Over the years I have been cajoled and vilified by my friends for being so liberal. A communist, a damn socialist. A person who, because of his beliefs during the Vietnam War, had no appreciation for what Americans stood for. You know, I was the odd man out. It was not malicious. It was just the way friends react to friends. We love each other. Unfortunately, politics always sorts us out into competing camps. My group of successful Armenian friends needed a liberal to beat up on and that was me. Most of it was in jest but my cousins always held true to their political beliefs.

The morning we arrived in Balboa we dropped off our stuff at Steven's house and walked a half a block to the beach. Most of the day we reminisced about the past. We caught each other up on our social and professional doings as well. By the time we got back to the house the inevitable political discussion came up. My cousin Jimmy could not contain himself. "Governor Jerry Brown is just unbelievable," he exclaimed. "He just couldn't accept President Trump's pulling out of the Paris Accord. He has to push far that carbon tax." Jimmy felt it would affect his trash collection business. And, trying to bait me, he continued, "and all the other crap that YOU liberals live by."

This is how it started. I held my tongue. I waited for the verbal avalanche to swallow me up. My conservative friend was in hyper speed. The conversation, obviously one way, moved to taxes. "You know, my God damn state income taxes are up to 13.8%." Jimmy shook his head in disgust. "With our high-income tax and our environmental laws, we are the least business friendly state in the country. I understand why all of our businesses are leaving California. Look at all the companies that are going to Texas. In fact, Shirley and I are thinking of moving to Nevada. No income tax over there! You have any idea what state income tax cost me?"

Before he could take a breath, another cousin broke in. "Shit, we worked all of our lives. Look how successful we Armenians are. We are like the Jews but for some reason they are liberal. I can't figure that one out. Anyway, I'm tired of paying all my hard-earned money for welfare for the God damn *Seves*." In Armenian, Seve is the word for blacks or African-Americans. I wondered how could I love these guys? They are such bigots. But, they are my cousins and it is more verbal than action!

These are really good people who are uncomfortable with diversity. For some reason they think they have the right to be bigots. I guess they figure they worked for the right to feel superior or something like that. If they can be successful and not a drag on society, why can't others do it as well? Quickly, another cousin chimed in. He started to talk about welfare and how everybody takes advantage of us taxpayers. "You know, the makers in the takers. The *Mexicoties* just keep having babies," referring to people of Mexican origin. He went on, "We have to pay for them. The more they have the more money the government gives them. I read somewhere they get 600 bucks a kid. And, none of them work or have insurance. Look at what they're doing to the cost of hospitalization! You know how much money it costs to have *those people* go to the emergency ward of a major hospital? And, what about the educational costs for those illegal immigrants?" I thought to myself, the Hawk, the cousin who was now talking, would probably start discussing the federal debt if he could spell it. I guess that is elitist of me, but I was feeling beat up by then.

I wanted to say something, but I knew that would start an argument. One of my other cousins saw how frustrated I was getting and he started to laugh. "I know what you're thinking," he said looking directly at me. "You want to say something. You are outnumbered partner!" He smiled. "We all voted for Trump. He holds all the answers." I could not help thinking, how can you follow a man who is a reflexive liar whose first intuition or reflex is to lie? Trump does not even know the truth when it is right in front of him! And, when you compulsively lie there is no chance for deliberation. There are no real solutions to real problems if you don't think things out. My thoughts were interrupted when my cousin continued, "Don't you liberals see that!"

Although I was in deep thought, I could still hear him. "You liberals are killing us! Remember when you thought integrating schools through bussing would somehow bring about integration? Did you see the *Los Angeles Times* article about the LAUSD? Only 7% of the kids in the district are white. Shit, all the white kids either moved or went to private schools. You guys are so screwed up ... look and see what your liberal ideas have done! I honestly think the school district is more segregated today than 30 years ago. You liberals have made it hard to live in California. Look at the crime. The minorities are out of control." I knew the onslaught was not over. As usual, I just shook my head. I knew it would not make any difference if I argued. He started in again, "I bet you like that guy who used to play for the San Francisco 49ers - the guy who wouldn't even stand up for the national anthem. And all the Black Matters shit." I was still quiet. I thought to myself, his name is Colin Capernick. I finally said something. Looking at my six friends, I said, "Come on. I don't want to get into this stuff. You won't change and I sure as hell won't buy into the crap you pick up on Fox News or wherever you get it ... so let's eat." We all laughed. I looked at my cousins and thought at least we were consistent having the same political divide since we were kids.

We are really not cousins but we have been together for more than 50 years. Our kids are not as close as we are. I do not know our children's politics but I am sure they are as closed-minded as we are.

However, I am sure they spout the same alternative facts that come from fake news the way we do. I am sure the stuff I heard from across the table is the same stuff they hear when they get together. I am sure my friends are disgusted when they think my vote cancels out theirs. And, vice versa! I am sure that it is the same for their kids and mine. For us, as a group of friends, or a clan, or what we affectionately call, *cousins,* politics just rolls off our backs. It is important, but our relationship is more important. We know we have each other's affection no matter what our political views are. We will always be there as a family in the good or the bad times. Even though politics are close to our hearts, family and friends come first. I wish that were the case with all people in this country. I wish Americans would view each other as *cousins*. But, they don't! People get caught up in alternative facts and false equivalents. They want to bolster their arguments with strangers to protect what is dear to them at the expense of others. Something is wrong. There is so much animosity between people. Especially in an age where we have so much information at our disposal. Collectively, we should be able to do better for our society. Things are screwed up. Things are just not right!

On the way home, I thought to myself, "I had a great time. My cousins have always been there for me. They are my family. My anchor. But, how can such good guys be so far off? How can they be so ill informed?" I started to laugh like my cousin Jimmy because I knew they felt the same way about me. They were probably thinking, "How can he be so off base?" We are at an age when all

this political drama doesn't much matter. We
are established and financially bulletproof. It
is our kids and the younger generation that we
pass the baton to that bothers me. They will be
the first generation of Americans who will be
poorer than their parents. We did not do a
good job. Some of us have so much and so
many more people are barely getting by. I will
attempt to explain why and how alternative
facts and untruths have brought us to this
crossroad. We can be inert and reactionary and
try to "make America great again" and fight to
stay pat. Or, we can move on to a new
inclusive America that is more opportunity
driven and equitable. This is the dilemma we
face. What do we do? Where do we go from
here?

Alternative Facts #1

I want to talk about the contentious political and social climate that is pervasive throughout all socioeconomic strata in the United States. The landscape of America is a microcosm of the world at large. Every democratic nation is facing huge political divides. Populist movements are being precipitated by the old political guard's inactions to the common person's problems. The United States is the leader of the developed world. Our cultural and economic ways of life are closely copied by progressive leaning countries. Our culture and political structure are the template for the richest and most powerful market driven economies. What we do, the world follows. For the most part, the world is America centric. I will paint a picture of America in my own words to show the reader who we really are and what problems we face. Let me start off by comparing conservatives with liberals. They are at odds. Please note the rich and conservative elements of society are defender of property rights. They defend the rights of ownership of material wealth. Charles Beard's book, <u>The Economic Interpretation of the Constitution</u>, sets forth a cogent argument for conservative political philosophy. Liberals or progressives are the champions of civil rights. This can be defined as defending voting rights, freedoms of sexual preference, gender rights and equity of income through equal opportunity. These are Jeffersonian, or Progressive, ideas.

I will discuss the difference between

these political views and how they are driven by alternative facts. Pedagogy, applied linguistics, is an important form of presenting these competing ideas. For that purpose, I will personalize my feelings on all matters political and social. In academia, the usage of the word I is, at best, showy. It is arrogant. At worst, as is the case today, it is a form of self- aggrandizement predicated on words not deeds. Using the first person sets up a simple ad hoc argument: who in the hell are you? Unless you are regarded as an authority or person of undeniable repute, using a first-person argument is foolhardy. Taking that as a given, let me talk a little about myself. I describe myself as an old fool. I am an academic. I taught at the community college as well as a State University in California for almost five decades. Neither institution is an academic powerhouse. Long Beach City College and California State University Long Beach, where I taught, are not top tier schools. I am not a person of academic or political repute. Saying I believe, I think, is setting myself up to be dismissed as an arrogant crackpot but I will take the chance. Academic or professional reviews of ideas have historically weeded out nut cases and self-promoters. Snake oil salesmen cannot meet the rigors of academic or scientific review. It is my belief that phrases like these have no place in public discourse unless they are based on provable truths. My opinions mean nothing unless rooted in verifiable facts and, therefore, it is important that I present my views in a truthful manner.

There is a phrase to describe people

who will lie to make a political point to protect their self-interests. They are BITTER ENDERS. They are so self-righteous and pious they will never accept the truth. They will make up lies, change history, bully, or cajole to get their way. They will never compromise! They have no allegiance to the truth. They would die before accepting something other than their version of what is factual or real. They are bitter and intractable to the very end. Nothing can move their needle. This must change if we are to be a democracy. It is of the greatest importance to be objective and open minded! We cannot be bitter enders and harbor hatred. We must forge a new path and put truth over opinions and alternative facts. We must view politics as a personalized extension of morality. People who lie, cheat, and steal to gain power are immoral. They use the tool of alternative facts. We must dull this tool through truth.

Let me broach the subject of political voice based upon facts. America is in a state of contentious competing ideas. People are frightened. There is social uncertainty and economic instability. Conservatives want to go back to yesterday. They view change as a negative. Liberals, on the other hand, view change as progress. In their view with change there is an opportunity for a betterment of our lives. Advancements in science and increases in technology create change. Liberals and conservatives view change differently. People look for truths to temper their fears of instability and uncertainty. Thus, the necessity of facts. The problem is in the marketplace of ideas, alternative facts are gaining credibility. There is an atmosphere of untruths. There is intellectual dishonesty. Out and out lies are being created to compete with truths. Just watch or listen to political pundits of all political persuasions. Fact check them! Using alternative truths and relying on one's opinions to suggest validity is woefully the fare of the day. Everyone has an opinion. The problem is everyone wants to project their opinion upon you. Not only express opinions but subject you to theirs. The other side will only measure you in their eyes leaving no room for compromise. Baseless opinions rule the political and social environment we live in. The problem is, falsehoods hold a tremendous sway with the general public.

Alternative facts or alternative truths must be called what they are. They are unacceptable LIES based on a social or political agenda of increasing one's leverage or power over others. These LIES have the ability to topple societal paradigms. They are the snake's venom that brings paralysis and eventual death to all we hold sacred and pure. I believe the public at large accepts falsehoods. The public at large is self-righteous, intractable and will not dignify other people's views. Most people use an a la carte approach to reality. You simply pick your own facts or what you think are facts to suit your needs.

For most people this is the least painful way to assimilate knowledge. The lowest hanging fruit as it were. Most people are culturally, politically and nationalistically inert. I also think as a society we are addicted to anxiety. We like turmoil as long as there is a solution or someone to make things right. We love a strongman type authority to ease our concerns. Believe it or not, anxiety creates a certainty. It is also entertaining! The problem with falsehood or alternative truths is they are harmful to others. Accepting alternative to reality calcifies the legacies of racism, sexism, and other injustices.

Please indulge me for a moment. I will use the dreaded I word again. I will be explicit in presenting my personal agenda. I am bias in my approach in attacking alternative truths. I am a Progressive. By using this political persuasion, I can dispel some of the disingenuous dialogue that the American citizenry faces. In the halls of governance, may it be the local, state or federal, seats of power abound. Both sides want power. Both sides lie! I am liberal. I am Progressive. You may view my take on things to be based on falsehoods but I will try my best to always be honest. My take on alternative facts will be viewed through a radical's lens. I am confident my left leaning foil will cut deep into the insidious lies that litter our social and political landscape.

As is the case with many Americans, the election of Donald Trump has been upsetting to me. It was a disappointment of epic proportions. The changing of the political guard usually brings about marginal effects upon the electorate. For most Americans, change is slow. However, for the people on the margins, it can be lightning fast. If Trump's or the Republican health bill passes, millions of Americans will not have medical insurance. That represents the accelerated change I am forecasting. The poor get poorer and the rich get richer at a faster pace than what befalls the middle class. Historically there have been many checks and balances to ill-gotten power (power based upon lies).

It will be my contention that Trump and the elk of people around him are trying to bring about quantum market driven change through lies. I will accept that these changes may even promote economic growth. However, the type of economic growth that Trump wants only leads to worsening levels of income distribution. The rich will pray upon the masses by lying and manipulating the truth. We all lie and manipulate the truth but the rich have more resources and, therefore, are more successful at it. Trump's place in the American history of the presidency should not be dismissed as an anomaly. He is the new face of much that is wrong with society today. On a personal note, would you be proud of him if he were your son? Do his personal traits of honor, loyalty, and integrity meet the historical standard of someone we should look up to? The classical Christian thinker, Evagrius Ponticus, is credited with writing about the seven deadly sins or capital vices: pride, greed, lust, envy, gluttony, wrath and sloth. These were not attributes that followed past presidents. People might not have liked Reagan, the Bushes, Clinton, or Obama but they were not viewed as bad people. Trump is different! He is truly dangerous. He is sinful and gluttonous in Christian terms. View his humanity relative to capital vices of the church. Is this what we expect of a leader? Does he have the visions we want to follow? He is an elitist by birth and a fascist by the encirclement of his upbringing.

His example of success is his father, Fred Trump, who was mendacious and manipulated people for his own welfare. He was a self-promoting exploiter of the values that American's hold dear. His real estate empire was discriminatory and exclusive. Trump himself was a slum landlord who evolved into a highly leveraged profiteer. Not much different than his father. People like the Trumps and their offspring will LIE, steal, and cheat to impose their elitist values upon society. They believe they have a superior pedigree as exposed by Alfred Pareto. They believe that 90% of the wealth should be held in the hands of 5% or less of the population. They believe in oligarchical rule. Look at his cabinet. They are wealthy like-minded people whose only accomplishment is having wealth. They feel they should be the developers and gatekeepers of our social and political doctrines. Their only skills are in making money. I will suggest that this skill is not transferable to governing others. These people believe theirs' is the only truth even if it leads to an 'Us vs. Them' social tension. The us in their case is the uber rich which opposes the majority of middle and low-income earners.

I want to digress for a moment. Most politicians lie and Trump is at the high end! In our history there has been what I call situational lying: Clinton, "I did not have sex with her"; President Johnson's made up a case for going into the Viet Nam War, the Gulf of Tonkin Resolution; John F. Kennedy being depicted by the press as a family man. These are all situational lies. There are many more that come to mind and they, for the most part, are situational. But, Trump is different! His lies are continuous. The cross all circumstances. For Trump, lying is applicable to any form of social intercourse. All situations in his personal and professional hemisphere have to be winnable no matter how aberrant his position. He will lie about anything from small to big to get an advantage to   further his influence or power. Everyone to him is an interloper. Every state of affairs is adversarial. He is a sociopath. His set of alternative facts are tools to better his position on everything or anything. He has no real values other than personal gain. Trump has no integrity. He feels no personal or social consequence for his actions as long as he bests someone through negotiations. Everything to him is a negotiation and he sees life as a set of hurdles that must be negotiated. He views life as a static me vs. them. One war after another based on arbitrage. He bases everything on lies. He creates a vortex of lies to get his way. This is disheartening. But, what is more disheartening is how many people buy into his pathology. The basic question of this book is why? What is wrong with our society? What is wrong with us that so many people covet a liar to get our own way?

Now, let us get back to me. I am in the top 1% of the wealth holders or stakeholders in America. My wife's and my income are in the mid six figures. We pay more than $200,000 a year in state and federal taxes. We are either the richest of the poor or the poorest of the rich. I am old. I am white. I am well educated. I described myself as being bulletproof to the changes that will accompany the governance of Donald Trump. Pejoratively, let's just say I'm able to adapt.

In the chaos that will befall most Americans with the Trump administration there is opportunity for a small percentage of the population. Other people's problems create openings for people like me to enhance my wealth and power. I gather information by being with the movers and shakers as it were. My circle of friends and acquaintances are the best and the brightest. My fiscal goals are simple. I need to protect my wealth and increase its value relative to others. That is contrary to the goals of the masses to accumulate wealth. Our desires are polar opposites. Economic wealth and political power are a zero-sum game. People like me are winning while the great majority of people are losing. As Donald Trump has said, we are the Bad Dudes. It is not personal. "Us vs. You" is the economic reality of competition.

This brings me to a point of internal conflict. The fact is, I protect myself and my standing at the expense of people below me. I want lower taxes, a bigger carbon foot- print and, of course, the ability to consume to my heart's content. The problem with me wanting to pursue my own self-interests is, in a zero-sum game, some will lose as I gain.

Russell C. Arslan

Alternative Facts #2

I will now endeavor to explain the sociological reasoning for the decay of the American dream. I will use the term emulate. Then, I will use the phraseology, "you cannot protect yourself." First, let me explain the concept of emulation. It was developed by Thorstein Veblen in his classic book written in 1899, <u>The Theory of the Leisure Class</u>. We will define emulation as an effort to match another person's achievement, typically by imitation. It can also be described as an effort or desire to equal or excel in appearance. In both cases, you are acting as a fool. You are not presenting the true substance of your being. You are projecting yourself as someone you are not. A good example of emulation is a young man who perceives he is a better athlete than he actually is. My example might seem far-fetched, but it reflects a profound truth about misreading our abilities. Assume you are a young African-American high school basketball player. This is a generality, a simplification, an over statement. We will discuss it later but in the black community, athletics are seen as a way to get out of poverty. Over 90% of the players in the National Basketball Association are African American. You decide to give up your educational track in school to play basketball which is a common dream of young men all over the country. You think you can be a future NBA All-Star. Four or five hours a day are spent playing basketball at the local gym. You are on the high school team and play AAU basketball rather than learning how to read and write. You give up academics for athletics! As I said, you think you have a chance of making it into the NBA. As a high school senior you are 6'1" tall and weigh 180 pounds. You average 14 points, 4 rebounds and 4 assists a game. You don't make all league nor all city honors, but you are better than the average high school basketball player. You enter a community college to fulfill your dreams of playing basketball. You play there for two years and are considered a marginally good player. Your coach helps you get a scholarship to a Division III school. Your chances of making it into the NBA are minuscule at best. You've given up academics for a dream. You barely make it through school, but you work out 5 to 6 hours every day. What you don't understand is you overestimated your skill level because, in truth, you are a rinky-dink division III basketball player.

Players in the NBA number less than 500. Besides being finely tuned athletes of superior physical fitness, they are, for all intent and purpose, glandular freaks. They are bigger, faster, and stronger than you. Thinking you are better than you are in absolute terms promotes a situation whereby you do not have the skills to compete with better athletes. Not only do you fail to make it to any professional level, you have lost your desire to recapture your lost education. The number of people who go back to school is small. In effect, for the rest of your life you are damaged goods. You made a bad choice. You pursued an athletic career which you could never fulfill. Most people will never recover from this folly of emulation. For many of you this is a harsh example. Using the term "damaged goods" is unsettling but it is true. This young man ended up with no salable skills.

Most Americans are dreamers, never to fulfill their dreams. The problem is they do not obtain competitive skills because their dreams come first. There are other simple examples. The young Caucasian boy in Appalachia who spends all of his money buying a pickup truck that has a gun rack. His efforts go into hunting and drinking not education. Many in his world become meth users because they see no future. Another example is the young boy or girl in the ghetto who spend their monies on tattoos and bling, not books. All of the above examples are forms of emulation because people are humiliated by, or ashamed of, their station in life. I have presented arguments in what is called arguing by exaggeration. By making things bigger, it shows clarity. Many young people give up a future for an unattainable present. People do not know what it takes to compete. In general, people do not meet their potential. There are a host of reasons for failure. It is important to note unsuccessful people's failure is the gain of successful people. It is a zero-sum world.

Let met talk about people in general. I will classify people into 6 major groupings. The first group is the POOR. In reality, the vast majority of people that are poor fall into two major categories. They are either under 6 or over 60 years old. The second group of people are the UNSKILLED WORKERS. Their labor makes them enough money just to survive. Then we have the SKILLED WORKERS or the vast majority of the middle class. Compared to the rich their incomes are meager. We now have BUSINESS PEOPLE. For the most part, they are failures but some do succeed. The few who are successful live good lives but do not consider them wealthy compared to the rich. The last group of workers are the PROFESSIONALS: the doctors, the lawyers, and the highly skilled technical class. We now come to the final group, the RICH. They don't have to work because their money does it for them. Each of these groups, except the rich, emulate groups above them. We look up to every group above us and try to image their lives at the expense of ours. We are out of sorts relative to our skills and importance. We think we are more valuable than we really are. Only the rich are emulated. Try to make it a personal practice to not emulate others.

I now want to explain the concepts of emulation through what is called occupational stratification. I will illustrate this by a simple diagram and will begin by talking about the poor. A simple way of looking at the poor is viewing them as people that have an income below the poverty line. The poverty line is a measurement of the lowest level of economic activity that is needed for an adequate standard of living. It is arbitrarily definitional and targeted to either individual regions or individual countries. In the case of the United States for the year 2015, the poverty line for a family of four is $24,250 per year. For an individual it is $11,770 a year. These statistics are derived from a number of government agencies: The Commerce Department, the Department of Agriculture, the Census Bureau, and the Department of Health and Human Services. In unsophisticated terms, the poverty line is calculated in the following way. The major purchase of a poor person or a family will be in the form of food. Food purchases will represent anywhere from 40 to 45% of a family spending if they are in the bottom quartile of income earners. An adult person needs 2,200 calories a day of a balanced diet. Dietary items are made up of the 5 major food groups with a balanced diet comprised of vegetables, fruits, grains, meats, and dairy products. The cost of these items for a family of four is approximately $200 to $220 a week. The other $280-$300 a week of income goes to shelter, transportation, clothing, taxes, etc. The money generated to purchase these items has to come from somewhere. It can be generated by people who make the minimum wage or less or it can come from government subsidies at local, state, or federal levels. It can also be generated through illegal activities. In any case, the poor do not have a lot.

If you are poor, your income comes from what other people give you or what you earn yourself and these monies determine your station in life. There is an adage, you are worth what you can be replaced for. An example of this is you work at a car wash. You are low skilled. Your job description is detailing cars. You are competing with people of like skills who can offer their employment for less than you. Let me use a conservative right-wing argument. An illegal alien comes across the border from Mexico or some other Latin American country and he or she is willing to work for $5.00 an hour. This is many times what they can make in their home country. The unscrupulous owner of the car wash is willing to accept a falsified Social Security card as proof of citizenship and the illegal now has the papers necessary to work. This illegal determines your worth. The Mexican in this case has the same set of skills as the legal American and renders the same service. He or she determines the legal person's wage. If the Mexican is willing to work for $5.00 an hour, the American will not get the job for $5.01 or more. The only way a person is worth more is if they can differentiate themselves. They have to render a better service or produce more good and services per hour. These are the only ways a person in this example is worth more than $5.00 an hour. A lot of people hate Mexicans because they will work for less. As I said, from where they come from, $5.00 an hour is a lot of money. It is a fortune in some countries. So much so, illegals will virtually die to get to America. Wouldn't you do the same thing to feed your family and reap the benefits of opportunity?

Everything is relative. In the aforementioned example, competition does not care if you are legal or illegal. It does not care if you are brown or white. You could be out competed by a woman who only wants to work part-time to supplement her family's income. You can be out competed by a teenager who is working while going to high school. In all of the above cases, someone else has determined your wage. You are poor as defined by a poverty line even though you are working and working hard! You are doing all the right things, but you are unable to receive a living income because what you do is easily replaceable. The market determines your value. You get what you are worth, not what you think you should get paid for your labor. I will make a case later about wages and government regulated market. In this example, we are talking about unfettered capitalism which, in colloquial terms, means less government interference. There are greater chances of one's income being diluted in unregulated markets. For now, I will just say, you are worth less because you are lacking the proper skills to warrant more.

We know what determines a poor person's worth. Now, let us reflect on what it means. Your mobility from the poorest of the poor to the richest of the poor still leaves you poor. It does not matter that in absolute terms, people at the lower end of the socioeconomic scale have made some progress over the years. Although the type of shelter, food, skill levels, and other variables have advanced, for the poorest segments of our population, they have not advanced by much over the last 200 years. There is change but it is marginal compared to the wealthy. Here is where emulation comes in. People who are poor are aware of their social status and live with great personal insecurities. They need a vehicle that expresses self-worth. They have little, or no, self-esteem. They suffer from what I call the diseases of despair. Some are dealing with drug problems both their own and in the community which they live. Areas where poor people live are disproportionately violent. Their view of the world is provincial and myopic. The vast majority of poor people do not believe in anything that might mitigate their circumstances. Their chances of getting out of insular poverty are minimal. Maybe 6% to 8% of poor people ever change their circumstances. In reality, what I will call the hard way out, one would need to increase their skill level. However, because of institutional discrimination, there is a lack of resources going toward education and retraining in poor areas. The chances of increasing one's skill level is difficult.

Inherently, there are many cultural and social forces that will not allow people to be successful. People who are poor will drag down anyone who tries to be different and wants to break the chains of poverty. There are many social obstacles that prevent mobility as there is little outside help for the poor. Inadequate educational opportunities are real barriers to mobility. Inside cultural pressure to stay the same are heavy and real. It is difficult, if not impossible, for most poor people to climb out of poverty through their own efforts. As I said, 6 to 8%. There are few resources that poor people have control over and there is little at their disposal to make them more competitive in labor market.

Now I will discuss a false positive. I will discuss how many people deal with their circumstances. There is a simple way of dealing with the culture of abject poverty. A person may never obtain a salable skill set to climb out of poverty but they can emulate and, therefore, emotionally leave their scares and culture behind. A person can infer he or she is not poor. They can do this by simply acting cool or detaching from the realities around them. They develop their own lexicon. They can dress differently. They can infer they are important and that their lives matter. They need to become controlling of the little world they live in. They will do anything to intimate they are not poor. In simple terms, they are imitating other people but do not have the skill set to defend who they are portraying themselves to be.

The poor will do anything to offset the realities of being unimportant. In many cases, they will tattoo their bodies with symbols to emphasize their importance as tattoos can depict events that are supposed to be noteworthy. The garb they wear is different. It is flashier. It is more colorful. Poor people are often verbally louder to bring attention. They perceive themselves to be social iconoclasts. Their speech is slow as are their movements. Their outward mannerisms represent a reflection of a life of leisure that comes with wealth. They impose their cultural standards upon others to control their fiefdoms as if what they control has value. An example would be gangs in the inner city and their territorialism. From the richest of the poor to the poorest of the poor, they infer they are more than they are. In reality, they are not integrated. For the most part, they are uneducated. Many poor people have limited vocabularies of less than 1,000 words. In a most disparaging comparison, Coco the chimp has a vocabulary of more than 900 words. Poor people are not mobile. Many poor people, whether in the inner city or in the tranquility of Appalachia, have never ventured more than 1 to 2 miles from their homes. Sadly, the poorest of the poor are actually children. Too many have little to eat. They have little physical contact that allows them to thrive. They have little of anything. Looking at infant mortality rates, the poor are different. A disproportionate number suffer from alcohol syndrome while some are crack babies. Many suffer from protein deficiency. Their health is that of children from the third world.

The poor are not like us. They are not seen. The vast majority of Americans in the middle class and the minority of wealthy Americans never venture into poor areas. As Michael Harrington, author of <u>The Other America,</u> said, "the poor live in a hidden America." They are a problem that no one wants. It is cheaper to either sequester them or to give them limited welfare as a plantation type handout to manage them. Society does this in the lowest cost manner. If we wanted, we could help solve their problems. We could give them transfer payments. We could educate them. We could give them opportunities to learn a valuable skill. On a more negative side, we could incarcerate them or, finally, we could extricate them from society through eugenics cleansing. We as a society will always choose the least expensive cure. Today, because it is less expensive, people that are poor receive government subsidies. This might not always be the case in the future. As I said, the cheapest solution will always win out. Over time poor people rarely get off the roles of the poverty-stricken. It is too costly to allow them to reach their potential and be contributors to society as education and retraining are costly. Much more so than welfare. Zero-sum game again. People do not want to give up income to help others. Alternative lies about poor people's abilities keep them in their place. As

I have said previously, it is virtually impossible to for them to get out of insular property. That is not because they are inferior but, rather, because they are brought up in an environment that does not allow for upward mobility. As an aside, by the grace of God, where you are brought up and who your parents are the major determinant of your success.

The picture of the poor that I have presented should be upsetting. But, and there is always a but, people are not upset because there is alternative truth. We lie about the poor to push for our own gains. Remember, it is a zero-sum game. The poor accept their plight because of emulation. People in general do not want to deal with them because it costs too much. Poor people do not have a political base that makes them relevant. The poor have been depicted as lesser human beings. They are poor because they're lazy. Blacks, in particular, are vilified and categorized by a history of untruths. They are portrayed as being inferior. Smaller brains and other harmful alternative facts. They are too sexual. They have too many children they cannot take care of. They are violent and dangerous. All of these designations are alternative truths. They are LIES! They are pure and simple LIES that make blacks more vulnerable and enslaves them into poverty. These same lies have been said of most minorities in America. Women, gays, immigrants, and countless other are discriminated upon by lies. In a nutshell, they are depicted as not being worthy to be part of the fabric of white Christian America. Hundreds years of lies and alternative truths have relegated the poor to a position of inferiority. They are poor because of economic, religious, and cultural bias. People use to say "bias of the past," but it is prevalent in today's reactionary environment.

People are born into poverty not by choice but by an insidious discrimination that is perpetuated by lies. The lie that all one has to do is work hard to get out of poverty is just that - an unmitigated, historical lie. There are historical facts and truths that show that a lack of individual economic and social mobility is promulgated by historical prejudice. The vast majority of people who live in poverty are not there by their own choosing. They are poor because of the overlord. Not all people who are causally related to the plight of the poor are necessarily bad people. They can be the unskilled worker who is threatened by people who have their same skill level. Poor whites at a car wash might be out competed by what they consider to be the dregs of society. Who hate and fears poor people more than unskilled rednecks? The one percenters that discriminate against the people below them do it to protect their income. They do not want to pay taxes to help others. They made it, so why help people that are lazy? The big lie again. From the richest of the poor to the poorest of the poor, it is virtually impossible to move into a higher socioeconomic stratum. No person should have a birthright such that they cannot progress up the economic ladder. But, poor people do! That is the case because of a lack of opportunity perpetuated by alternative facts and lies. It is a zero-sum game where 15 to 20% of the population is relegated to the lowest economic stratum.

Alternative Facts #2A

Some quick thoughts. When I talk about the proclivity of people in different social strata, I will be generalizing. When I will discuss a person or groups of people's activities, I will use generalities. I will say people are exclusive, they are greedy, etc. It is important to understand that I am fully aware that most people's actions are not cognitively recognized. Most people do not think things out. They react. I will be making mention of the wealthy. Using terms like, "rich people." They do not sit behind a mahogany desk and plan how their activities will affect the social well-being of others. They do not say, "Watch this. Here is how I am going to take advantage of black people or illegal aliens." They do not plot the demise of lesser people. There are exceptions, but they are rare and hopefully not eventful. There are reactionary people and plotters of social policy, but they are louder of mouth than actions. In actuality, most rich people are protecting their heritage or status, which can also be said for all social stratum. Most people never think of the consequences of their actions.

In the following example of occupational stratification, when I say that rich people are acting in a greedy self-promoting fashion, please remember they are not actively cognizant of the results of their activities. They are just seeking a better life for themselves and their families. In social terms, they might not be bad guys. But, and there is always a but, their actions might be harmful to society at large.

People are not necessarily aware of how they affect others. People that live in a laissez-faire manner are, in effect, saying, "no one has the right to tell me what to do!" ----- They usually believe your opinion is weak but, for the most part, they believe other people should have the right to have an opinion. If enough people have the same opinion, it can affect society. That is democratic rule. This can easily be offset by a wealthy person's opinion who has the ability to buy political favor which is accomplished through political action committees, soft money, and dark money. Money as a political voice is protected by the 2010 Supreme Court decision, Citizens United v. FEC. The rich have a greater voice. They, by definition, have more chips.

We all feel we have the right to be who we are. We know other people can be critical. We just do not want a system of governance that stops us from having the right of free speech. We do not want others to tell us how to live our lives. The trouble is, when there are alternative facts instead of truths it impairs our ability to make proper decisions and be who we really are. People do not think things out. They just protect their own self interests. This leads to social cannibalism. The problem is, rich people can bite deeper and harder into the social fabric. Through the dissemination of alternative facts and the ability to control political intercourse, the rich are an advantaged group. The problem is we make our decisions on alternative facts doled out by the wealthier class. We have few alternatives to untruths. We are misinformed. It will be my contention that this misinformation, or alternative truths, are controlled and disseminated by what I will call the proprietary class. Again, they might not sit behind a desk and plan things out, but their actions lead to a concretization of wealth and power. Let me relate some quick examples of important societal misconceptions. Polls show that over 60% of Republicans do not believe in evolution. There are still Holocaust deniers. There are climate change deniers. Hundreds of thousands of American children go unprotected from childhood diseases as their parents do not believe in vaccinations. None of these positions are backed by fact but someone gains from the dissemination of these untruths or out and out lies. One more example, a form of religious intolerance by someone of high political standing. I will talk about the Vice President of the United States, Mike Pence. Vice President Pence actually feels that homosexuals can be re-programmed to be heterosexuals. He demonizes them as being lesser, evil, and aberrations. He has on many occasions talked about incarcerating them for their sinful ways of life. This is just an example of alternative truths or misinformation. His misguided understanding of sexuality gives him power and control over what he fears. His biblical interpretation leads to discrimination and harm and this should be unacceptable in the 21st century. People who believe this, for the most part, are not bad people. Pence might not be a bad person. I can be pleasant and call him ill informed. Or, I can be honest, and call him stupid and mean spirited. In either case, his actions cause pain to others. In any event, he has the right to his own opinion.

However, he should not have the right to determine how you or I live. The same can be said about abortion or the environment.

Emulation, which we are discussing, is based on untruths and people aspiring to be more than they are. People want an easy way to gain respect and the riches that our society can bestow upon them. As I said before, there is no grand scheme or design by the rich to do the common person harm. The misnomer that opportunity will allow people to gain a greater share of wealth for the most part is just that, a misnomer. I contend we live in a zero-sum game. If somebody gains, it will be at our expense. People act in a laissez-faire manner to maximize their own self interests. This creates an "Us vs. Them" mentality which, for the most part, is injurious to everyone other than the rich. The game is rigged. The game is unfair. But, I must stress, the rich do not intentionally plan this out. Things happen because we get out competed. The rich pass on their political thoughts through their profit seeking media machines. The problem with this is where we gain information to live by. It is not their fault that we accept what they throw at us. There is enough information and there are enough truths for us to make proper value judgments which will not be harmful to us. If we are too lazy or, worse, not caring enough, then in the long run it is our fault to have lesser standing in society. If we emulate its consequences are our fault.

I will get back to the concept of occupational stratification and tie this general notion with the concept of emulation. By tying these two ideas together, it will give us a good starting point for looking at the effects of alternative facts or truths.

Again, I believe that seeking one self-interest
by pursuing laissez-faire activities creates a
situation that results in a zero-sum game.

41

Alternative Facts #3

Previously I mentioned the poor as a societal group. Now, I will talk about the next strata, the unskilled worker. They emulate just like the poor. They infer they are something they are not. This is because of the same insecurities that befall the people below them. By definition, the unskilled workers have no skills. They cannot protect themselves in the marketplace from the uneducated or other people with no skills. They are afraid of the masses below them. They are scared and frightened and unapologetic of their fear. Rage and hatred towards the poor displace their fear. The only thing that differentiates the unskilled from the poor is the fact that they are employed. Most of the unskilled workers are white and do not face the same level of institutional discrimination as poor people of color. The worst thing that can be said of them is they are Poor White Trash. Of all of the designated income strata, the unskilled are the most insecure. They have enough income to see what they want. They are close enough to material wealth to want it but they do not have the requisite skills to generate enough income to meet their material desires. Let me exemplify this by a simple example of deflection in job market. A janitor outwardly pronounces him or herself to be a maintenance engineer. They hope that by donning a title upon themselves they will be more acceptable and will be respected by the community at large. A garbage collector emulates by calling him or herself a sanitary engineer. Both categories of workers are saying, "Look at me - I am more important than my actual job." To them, titles infer they are more valuable than what they really are. They will spend greater proportions of their incomes to obfuscate who they are. They will spend too much money on clothing and material objects relative to their meager earnings. In colloquial terms, they are trying to keep up with the Joneses. In reality, they do not have the income to do it. They will imitate what wealthier people do at the expense of their saving and will forgo savings that gives them security in the future. Their spending habits, lying about what they have, and a false description of what they do, misrepresents their place in society. Pure and simple, they are replaceable. Replaceable by the very people they hate and despise. No one is more reactionary than the white unskilled worker. Their fear of the poor is somewhat justified because they can be out competed by lowest stratum of our society. For them, instead of obtaining greater skills than the poor, it is easier to discriminate against them. It takes too much time and effort to better someone's skill level and hating them and keeping them down is easier.

Let's get back to a description of what these people do in the workplace. Job title in both of the above cases is no more than a social deflection of one's insecurities. Title trumps actual remuneration. Pushing a broom or emptying garbage cans are just what they appear to be. They are work for beasts of burden. They are physical endeavors that are not predicated upon mindful skills. They can be done by any able person of like physical stature. The unskilled worker has no protection. Our simple rule of determining wealth was that you are as valuable as what you can be replaced for. Hence, the unskilled worker is defenseless to the masses of unemployed people. They are defenseless to the minorities who they hate - defenseless against people who will work for less. We will later show how capitalism cannot employ the masses. Profit seeking alone cannot feed, house, or employ the multitude of people in America. Our economic system creates institutional shortages that promotes competition between occupational stratum.

The unskilled worker, no matter how he or she dresses or what they call themselves, are hateful and frightened of the poor. No matter how they try to portray themselves they can be out competed by the very people they hold in contempt. To make one feel better there is always a whipping boy. If there are people who are inferior to you, you are, by definition, better. The unskilled are vocal and physically threatening towards people they considered to be challenging their economic position. Law and order come to mind. Have the police create a social order to concretize your hierarchical position. Police do not stop and frisk white people. They stop and frisk black people. They do not hassle heterosexuals. They hassle homosexuals. They do not stop people who wear acceptable garb. They stop people who look different. Police are more differential to men they are women. Law and order maintains cultural norms. Today's unskilled workers are no more than yesterday's moral majority. They feel comfortable in the social norms of 200 years ago. Their religious authority, as they call it, is exclusionary of people they think are below them. The unskilled worker is frightened of change. They are ultra conservative in political leaning. By definition they are uneducated, maybe a high school degree. Most importantly, they are self-righteous. They are hateful arrogance minions. They follow the disingenuous populist diatribe of people like Donald Trump. Most of them are Christians, Southern Baptists or Evangelicals. These so-called people of faith have a deep hatred for people who can replace them in the marketplace. They are hateful and hypocritical. They block every entrance of mobility for people below them to protect their wealth. They feel the world is a zero-sum game. In reality, they are vulnerable because they have no skills. They have personalized their hate towards the people they feel are competing with them for jobs. They have disdain for people who they perceived to be less fortunate. Again, here come the alternate truths. They have bought into the conceptualization that poor people are poor by choice. Poor people are either inferior by birth or have a lackadaisical purpose of life. Mental acumen and adaptability are not in the wheelhouse of the unskilled worker. Besides hatred for the poor, they revel in the past where the world was based on sheer physical labor. "Make America Great Again" is their anthem. Their skill sets are antiquated. They are many years behind technology and, as a group, they do not read. Their knowledge base is decades behind technology. Most unskilled people gather their information from either hearsay or long- standing customs. Their knowledge base is not in conformity with present-day social and economic paradigms. They do not view education as a benefit. They do not partake in training to meet the needs of the new world of technology. An example would be a coal miner whose skills are predicated upon brute force. Structurally, the industry they are in is dying. No matter what Donald Trump says, coal will never come back. There will be no jobs for coal miners in the future. The miners hate environmental controls because they perceive them as threats even though there are greater threats to their jobs. They are so ill informed that they do not consider technology or alternative fuel sources as the real reasons they are losing their jobs. I will discuss these threats in a moment. In sociological terms, the unskilled hate change and anybody that is different than them. Blacks, gays, people of a different faith, and people that are purportedly smarter or more intellectual than them are viewed as threats. In their lives, there is a need for sameness and order, however, it is a life of past generations not only in deeds but in thinking. They are unskilled and feel unprotected. Emulation and hate give them since of protection.

The heartland of America is made up of the unskilled. For the most part, they are white males, older, and ill informed. Their women follow their men's paces. Women may actually be more frightened and hateful than the male counterparts. They are reactionary and covet the old ways. The parental family as a unit spreads its insecurities on to its children. The unskilled class --- regenerates itself with each new iteration as frightened as the last. The tribal slogan of "Make America Great Again" is apt. The unskilled perceive themselves as the heart and soul of America.

In reality, they are reactionary. They strive for the good old days that never were. Their future is static. In reality, the future is based upon precipitous change. People must change with the vicissitudes of a technological society. I had mentioned the coal miners before. They exemplify the unskilled worker. They try to impose their political wills to save their jobs. They are threatened by the multitude of people below them. In reality, the future holds that technology, not the poor, will replace them. They are willing to stop progress toward new forms of energy to protect themselves. They are willing to destroy the Earth to protect themselves. They denied the role of climate change. They are hateful emulators who profess their allegiance to Donald Trump. They, and the people below them, the poor, have the most to gain by being retrained and reeducated. But, and there always is a but, they are hardened like tempered steel when it comes to change. It is easier to emulate and willfully oppose the people below them than to meet the needs of a more technological world. Unskilled workers are not willing to put in the effort to upgrade their skills. It is easier to buy into alternative truths then protecting their own position through hard work and parsimony. If they did not buy into alternative truths and increase their own skill level, they would not have to be exclusionary at the expensive of the poor.

In summation, unskilled workers are not inherently bad people. They are just protecting themselves. The problem is their actions are the touchstone of repression. Their culture is ill-informed and built on weakness and retribution. They keep the poor under their thumb. They keep them in check. The culture of the unskilled worker does not allow for change in the social order. What they believe in is not equitable. They are exclusionary. Inherent in the culture of the unskilled is the expression of wrath. The self-righteousness of the unskilled worker is predicated upon their inherent low self-esteem and weak position in the labor market. Their hate and subjugation of the people below them is a construct of their hierarchy. What makes things worse is unskilled people have a great discomfort for disorder. To ameliorate their fears, they need certainty in lives and they willingly accept alternative truths. They are willing to accept anything that makes them feel superior to people below them. Alternative facts, lies, push the unskilled worker to emulate people of higher standing. The very people that unskilled worker looks up to are the same people that repress them. It is no different than the unskilled repressing and shutting off the poor. All doors or avenues of mobility are closed off by the socioeconomic strata above them. The unskilled worker, just as the poor, have a culture that is counter to their existence. Their culture, based on emulation and misinformation, will enslave them to people above them in the socioeconomic hierarchy of America.

Alternative Facts #4

Skills are required to be upwardly mobile in our society. They are also fleeting because of the dynamic nature of the economy. Today your skill set may be relevant and in demand yet tomorrow your skills may be obsolete. The ever-increasing knowledge base and its technological component necessitate keeping current and forward leaning. Skilled workers, the next group I will discuss, collect their skills through formal education. The higher-level skilled people, who derive their incomes from computer and electronics driven industries, have obtained their skills through formal training at colleges or technical schools. Many other productive skill sets are acquired in similar ways. People with skills in finance, engineering, environmental science, etc. are formally trained. Others acquire skills through a labor process similar to that of the guilds in the beginning of the Renaissance. The apprentice, journeyman, and, ultimately, the master, receive their skills through a long process. Carpenters, plumbers, electricians are colloquially called trades people. It takes years to master a trade.

This process extends to glass blowers or even magicians. Malcolm Gladwell, in his book, <u>Outliers</u>, developed a theory that it takes at least 10,000 hours to hone a person's craft. This measuring stick is applicable in our competitive marketplace for labor. It takes almost 5 years of training to reach what I will call, "a simple degree of excellence." Using a 40-hour work week times a 50-week year, works out to be a 2,000 hours year. Five years of work is the magic 10,000 hours needed to be good at what you do. The problem is, the world is not static. The world is dynamic. That means we must commit to more than 10,000 hours over our lifetime or we don't keep up with technology.

Let me explain. From the beginning of humankind, 2 to 2½ million years ago, the acquisition of knowledge has been a slow process. In what I call the primitive stage of society, all over the world, the acquisition of knowledge and technology came about at similar rates. This is called the collective unconscious. An example are the pyramids in Egypt and Central America. There is no known communication between the builders of the Great Pyramid in Giza, Egypt and the Mayans who built the pyramids at Chichen Itza in Mexico. Pyramids were important in both cultures. Technology and science were not transferred across the Pacific. Both civilizations developed the ability to build these massive undertakings on their own. This type of leap or change in science did not take place until approximately 10,000 years ago as, for the first 2 million years, there was little growth or advancement in the human condition. Prior to ancient China or Egypt, humans essentially looked the same. They acted the same. Their tools were the same. Archaeological studies show people's brains were similar in function. Anthropologists who have studied evolution have shown there was very little change in humans during the first couple millions of our existence. Life was predicated upon surviving in the harshest of living conditions and there was time for little else except trying to survive. In evolutionary terms, human advancement was slow. Almost 100% of a human's time was needed for survival. Humans had to fight back against the elements. Mortality rates were high and morbidity rates were low. As soon as humans had extra time, using 23 hours of effort per day to survive and the 24th hour could go to other activities, the human race would expand its knowledge base. It would have time for other endeavors. Humans now had the ability to pass on more information to other generations. As the time spent on survival lessened, the time available for social and intellectual pursuit expanded.

Let us fast-forward. As we needed less time for survival, the production of food and shelter started to increase at a faster rate. Humankind went from the primitive stage of social development to an agricultural stage. Humans harness the ability to produce an excess of foodstuffs. They could save food for future needs (stockpiling resources for the future). As time progressed, humans domesticated animals for consumption. As it took less and less time to meet our needs for survival (food and shelter), humans started to advance our knowledge base. This gave the human race the ability to understand nature and to perpetuate knowledge.

Let me try to tie this together. If we put all accumulated information in a book from the emergence of humans to approximately 1900 to 1920 it would be called <u>Volume 1</u>. The book would hold all of the technical and social information created by humankind. Our knowledge base as it were. The slow pace of knowledge at the beginning of our evolution was probably less than one 1,000th of percent per year. For all intent and purpose, humans were inert. By the early 1900's the accumulation of knowledge was growing at a rate of 3 to 4% a year. The accumulation of knowledge has accelerated to even a greater extent today. In one year, we can accumulate as much knowledge today as all humankind had accumulated over its history from our beginning to 1900. In today's technological environment, Volume 2 would only take 1 year to write. That book, which holds all of humankind's knowledge from our inception to approximately 100 years ago, could be replicated in 365 days. The important thing is to ask ourselves is what does this mean? It means knowledge is dynamic not static. Technology is dynamic not static. Therefore, skills must be viewed the same way. Not only are the needs for skills increasing they are becoming more sophisticated with greater degrees of specificity. This leads to the concept of greater opportunity costs in terms of training to be more skillful. Let us get back to the adage of you are only worth what you can be replaced for. To be skillful, to be less threatened by people around you, you need to obtain skills through an educational process. You need to be updated and trained on a perpetual basis.

With this being said, skill workers are worth more than the poor and unskilled workers at an ever-increasing rate. By definition, the poor and the unskilled are static. The dynamics of our economy force the skilled to update constantly. Keep this in mind. The unskilled can be replaced by the poor because they have the same technical levels. The skilled can only be replaced by people with a greater skill sets or by technology itself. Technology in a capitalistic

system is a labor-saving phenomenon.
Therefore, the skilled worker has two dragons
to slay. They are threatened by people below
them. They are also threatened by artificial
intelligence, robotics, and cybernetics. As is
the case with people below them, the skilled
worker must protect his or her position by
excluding other people from having their
skills.

They are fighting the wave of
technological change and suppressing others
from sharing in it. The skilled worker cannot
allow others to obtain their knowledge.
Exclusion is the fare of the day. Joining a
guild or a craft is tantamount to joining an
exclusive club. The process of apprentice,
journeyman, master is no more than a process
of whittling down the number of people who
will become skillful. Excluding the number of
people getting into a guild, the crafts, is
historically done by excluding people because
of sex, race, and ethnicity. I will call this a
form of tribalism. This exclusion creates a
higher value of anyone who makes it all the
way through the process. It lowers the number
of people with a skill therefore increasing
their value. It is interesting to note how
exclusion becomes historical and cultural.
There are not many female plumbers and for
years there were very few black firefighters
nor gay educators.

Exclusion is allowed for people to
protect their jobs and make larger sums of
money at the expense of others. It is a vehicle
for the degradation of all people below the
economic strata you are in. It is allowed for
the discriminatory and bigoted practices of
keeping other people down. This process for
skilled workers stepping down upon people

below them to protect themselves is no different than what the unskilled did to the poor. All of the exclusionary traits of the unskilled reverberate deeply into the skilled occupational strata. The skilled worker is no more refined nor are they safer than the people that they subjugate and exclude from sharing the bounties of economic progress. It is a zero-sum game.

We now know the skilled worker restricts others. They are exclusionary. The problem is they also fall into the trap of emulation. The tech guy graduates from a top-tier school, Caltech, MIT, or other major universities. They make a lot of money. In many cases, their salary starts in the low six figures. These new hires are close to the one per centers in income. In short order they want to act like they are more important to the business than they really are. They perceived their skill set, programmer, is as important as the entrepreneurial risk taker. They desired the same high-end car their boss drives - a Porsche, BMW, or the McLaren. They live in areas like Silicon Beach in Playa Vista where the housing market is essentially for the rich. They spend their money at the most expensive restaurants. They act as if they are more important to the company then the owner. In most cases, they spend money at the expense of their future. They feel bulletproof. In the high-tech industries like many other economic sectors in America, there are high rates of failure. This means that even the best of skilled workers will fall on hard times. These young people have not acquired nor updated their skills since they left the university setting. In most cases, they did not become more technological savvy over time. Instead, they became more corporately political. As their incomes rose because of political relationships within the corporate structure, their technical level dropped. By the time they are 35 to 40 years old their skill level is lower than entry-level employees. To gain more corporate recognition they traded their technical strengthens for corporate relationships. As they progressed up the corporate ladder, they became more vulnerable to being replaced. It is only a matter of time before that lower paid employee and new hires will eventually take their jobs.

Because of emulation, they think they are more valuable than the really are. They become arrogant. They think they could fall back on their personalities over their technical skills. By emulating the owners and politically schmoozing and not producing, they no longer can protect themselves from young cheap labor. They are acting counter to their own interests. In some cases, the artificial intelligence they skillfully created will replace them. They will be replaced not by a worker with equivalent skills who would receive less money but be replaced by technology.

It is ironic they would develop something that would take their job. IBM's Watson super computer is such an instrument. It is a labor killer. Automation, robotics, artificial intelligence, and cybernetics make humans replaceable. With the potential for workers to lose their jobs the concept of a "universal basic income" has become popular once again. The concept is simple. Cybernetics and automation are labor saving devices. If too many workers are displaced the effective demand for products is gone. Higher wages and government subsidies are left to create an effective demand if business is to stay viable. Income has to be distributed more equitably or the economic system comes to a halt. Massive dislocation of workers was first presented by Karl Marx in his 1867 book, <u>Das Kapital</u>. Universal income was later clarified in Joan Robinson's 1942 book, <u>An Essay on Marxian Economics</u>. Automation and cybernetics as a causality of unemployment were again visited by Norbert Wiener in his 1948 classic book, <u>Cybernetics</u>. The message is clear - skilled workers, even at the highest levels, cannot rest. Workers must be retrained and keep current with new technology on a continual basis. To do less will lead to being pushed out the door by some geek kid straight out of college or by technology. Not so much the geek kids but by new technology in the near future. Look at the potentiality of self-driving trucks. How many teamsters will lose their jobs? We need to take a hard read on technology and employment. Add this to emulation and the synergism portends a rocky future. To emulate, preferring the manager's office, is a formula for disaster in itself. Not being able to compete with technology is bad enough but if it is caused by emulation it is a lesson hard learned. The combination is toxic.

Let us get back to alternative facts. People that are high wage earners, low to middle level six figures, are mindful of and inundated with marketing and advertising. They are coddled by sellers of goods and services so they can spend beyond their means. This is done through insidious methods, alternative facts. The high-end wage earner spends too much money on present-day consumption. Consumption is always at the expense of savings. You cannot get rich without savings. Rich people increase their net worth not by consuming but, rather, by investing.

When skilled workers emulate the rich to show off their six-figure incomes it is counterproductive. The watch, the car, the club or the expensive restaurants are all window dressings to hide people's insecurities. Look at the low-level skilled worker. In this case, it will be the industrial worker at an auto plant in Michigan. A General Motors worker makes $60,000 to $70,000 a year. Their income is totally derived by the unionization process, the rule of exclusion to make a person more valuable at the expense of others. Most skilled workers have little or no savings. The pickup truck they purchased to express who they are, in some cases, the most expensive asset they own. Many skilled workers are renters not owners of the housing they live in. In keeping up with the marketing and advertising they see in the media they spend their wealth beyond their means. A $60,000 Ford 150 pickup truck fully loaded could be worth one third to one quarter of what their house is worth. That is not the ratio for wealthier people. Skilled workers are living a lie. You cannot afford the truck if you have to spend over and above your income. One of the major problems is the products skilled workers purchase depreciates at an accelerated rate. This is counter to wealthy people. When wealthy people purchase things, they historically increased in value.

A skilled worker wants his wife or daughter to be socially accepted. A nice watch is an important part of her jewelry. For the skilled worker, in this case a plumber, a Citizens watch, an Apple watch, or a Movado watch would be a high-end commodity. In the realm of watches, any of these watches would be considered lower to middle end. These type watches loose 80% to 90% of their value in a very short period of time. When a wealthy man wants to adorn his wife with a watch, it might be a Cartier or a Rolex. In truth, even these watches are second-tier watches but they do appreciate in value over time. There is a market for pre-owned high-end watches. They do not depreciate in value like the watch for the skilled worker's wife. When the autoworker wants to buy a car, he might buy a Chevy Tahoe for $45,000 to $50,000. The problem is, the SUV will lose up to 30% of its value as soon as he drives it off the dealer's lot. When a wealthy person wants to buy a nice SUV for his wife, it might be the $400,000 Bentley. As noted earlier most items consumed by the wealthy appreciate over time. They do not depreciate. There is a thriving market for used high-end vehicles. Buying into alternative truths force people to portray themselves in a higher economic stratum. The causal effect is emulation. In reality, the more you purchase to compete with wealthier or rich people the worse off you will be. These alternative truths are form of manipulation/propaganda created by a business class to make a profit. What we see or hear that motivates our consumption drive a wedge deeper between the rich and the people below them.

Alternative truths that state skilled workers are mobile is another lie. Alternative truths that purport skilled workers participate in profits for the most part are lies. They get fired first. Very few skilled workers generate high enough incomes that allow them to capriciously spend. No one gets rich by spending! People only get rich by investing which is derived from saving. If you buy into the big lie, that you deserve to have what the rich have, you will spend yourself poor! When poor, unskilled or skilled people are lied to or tricked into spending, it once again becomes a zero-sum game.

Alternative Facts #5

The next tranche (?), occupational stratum, or occupational level is the exalted business person. Let me begin by saying almost 90% of entrepreneurial endeavors end up in failure. Business people are the backbone of our economy, but it is a hard road to follow. They are the major creators of jobs in America. Most neophytes in the business world are not prepared. They are either underskilled or underfunded. They do not understand they are most often in a marketplace where they are set up for failure. That does not mean a person cannot be successful. It means that a new entry into the market is most often beset by less than acceptable results. To be successful most startups must venture into what is called a niche market. New businesses must out compete others with either greater nimbleness, a newer or better product, or a lower price. This is possible, but the chances of success are generally below 10%. Like the other economic strata we have talked about, there are many alternative facts the entrepreneur must wade through. The most important truth is that success is not only difficult but it is fleeting. Also, the fallacy that the marketplace is fair. In reality, nearly 85% of all goods and services produced in the United States are produced in an oligopolistic market. The top 1,000 business as measured by Fortune Magazine produce over 82% of our goods and services. One of the biggest untruths is that the marketplace images the writings of Adam Smith who was the father of capitalism. In 1776 he wrote <u>An</u>

Inquiry into Nature and Causes of the Wealth of Nations. The marketplace today is neither competitive nor is there free entry as it is portrayed in Smith's book. In a free marketplace, there is free entry and free exit. There are many buyers and sellers. Both the buyers and sellers are small and have no market influence. The products are homogeneous, not differentiated. These assumptions are not the case in today's economy. Entry is not always free. The cost of money, licensing costs, and governmental restrictions are impediments. There are only a few, not many, producers. The number of buyers can be restricted. The sellers are large and influential. The products are not all similar, they are differentiated. The real world is a hard place to compete. Alternative truths depict the market as a place where success is easily obtainable. However, it is not!

Small business people feel their chances of success are greater than the realities of the marketplace. Coming up with an idea is much easier than bringing that idea to market and succeeding against other competitors. Most people with entrepreneurial desires identify with the super-rich as if they are similar. The new entrepreneur feels he or she is going to be in the small club of success. They perceive themselves as the new Bill Gates, Elon Musk or Warren Buffett. They believe they possess the same entrepreneurial magic. In emulating the rich, they read the same magazines, Forbes, Fortune, or many or all of the entrepreneurial digests. They read the same newspapers, the Wall Street Journal or the New York Times. They watch the same financial analysis on

TV. They believe it is only a matter of time before they are successful and rich. They think they can see around corners like the successful people they emulate. They think they can understand the sophisticated nuances of business like their successful counterparts. They think they have the financial reserves to outlast market variations. In truth more than 80% of them fail in the first three years. But they still believe in the big lie. They believe the marketplace is lined with easy pickings. The big lie says they are on the road to riches and they will become successful in a short period of time. All it takes is hard work and good fortune.

Here comes the bad news. If they follow the dictates of tax policy, trade policy, or industrial policy that the rich advocate through government intrusion in the marketplace they will fail. Following the political goals of the rich is counterproductive to small businessperson's success. The small businessperson does in fact need government regulation. They need protection from the oligopolies and market makers. Small businesses need subsidies. Because of scale they are less efficient. They cannot compete with the mega stars who they emulate. One of the major problems is small businessmen believe they can penetrate the market. Market penetration coupled with long success is for the most part an unfulfillable dream.

Let me give you a simple example of the entrepreneur who will not face truth and buys into the big lie. He thinks and acts like a big shot. He thinks he is successful. Do not forget, it is all relative. He is not a bad person. He just has a higher self-regard than warranted; the slow death of emulating. He is a small businessperson, someone who has a startup business predicated upon an app. He is sitting at the dinner table with his family. One of his children has asked him how much money he made that year. This is a personal question even for a member of the family. A reaction will follow. The father pleasantly says to the son or daughter, "It's none of your business." He does it in a polite way. Another reaction could be the father tells them he makes an exaggerated amount. This made up sum will give the father greater respect at home. His children will feel better about their position with their friends. The father's responses are generally the second case. In this example, the son pushes further. He says, "It's not that I don't believe you Dad, but I would like to see your tax return." The father acquiesces and brings out his tax returns. He thinks $120,000 after taxes will quiet down his son. He is in the top 5% of income earners in the country. The son looks at him. He pauses for a second. "Is that all you make? I thought we were doing better." The father is enraged. He does not want to push it because the son has challenged his very being to the core. His son suggested that what he made was not enough. That he was a failure! He does not make enough to be considered a successful businessperson. He does not make enough to be a good father. This would be a damaging blow to any father! In the above example, notice I did not mention mothers nor daughters. It is evident that the marketplace is not equitable when it comes to gender. Let me get back to the father son dynamic. It is easier to lie to your son than be truthful. Most people hide behind emulation. It is easier until the truth catches up with you.

Now, let us look at the concept of emulation as directed by alternative fact or truths. People put themselves in a position of high levels of potential failure when they go into business ventures. Most sole proprietors who are measured against the mega-successful business people are overshadowed by multiple levels of wealth and power. The vast majority of sole proprietors have bought into the notion that they are risk takers and should be rewarded for it. They are special. They are more integral to the success of the business than the workers who actually make the good or service. So much better, they differentiate themselves with multiple time the income they pay their workers. They identify with being an entrepreneur not a worker. They have bought in the alternative truths hook, line and sinker.

The business class are relativity unsuccessful and emulate just like the people below them. Look at all the small business owners that go under every time we have a recession. They over spent or under saved for that rainy day. Acting like a big shot always has a way of catching up you. Here is an example. A young entrepreneurial type out of Stanford develops a new betting site that is legal throughout the entire United States. Within less than one year he has recovered his initial investment. He anticipates making $500,000 his first year. He feels comfortable and goes after the good life. He buys a house in Santa Monica near Silicon Beach. The house is modest but, at $1,300 per square foot, it still costs him almost $4,000,000.00. That is approximately $15,000 a month if he puts down $1,000,000.00 down. He needs a car worthy of a successful young businessman. He leases a Tesla which will cost $1,500 a month. His wife needs a car, which amounts to another $1,200 a month. And, the two kids MUST go to private school. Buckley is $36,000 a year per child. That comes out to $6,000 a month. They need clothing, food, and entertainment money. That is another $6,000 to $8,000 a month. Then, there is the family vacation. Even Hawaii for a successful businessman is $25,000 for a week. Our big shot will spend $30,000 a month. But, and there is always a but, there is always more and better for the young successful business types.

Bigger houses, nicer cars, greater vacations. It goes on and on. The economy raises and falls just like the tides. Good years always are followed by bad years. When the economy tanks, and it will, he will tank with it. He was not rich. He just made a lot of money. But, not enough to see him through bad times. His world came down like a house of cards. He emulated. He paid the price. This is not a one off. It is symptomatic of the small businessman.

Alternative Facts #6

The next level of occupational stratum is the professional. Historically they have been lawyers, doctors, and people with extensive professional training. There are many subsets of professionals. In all cases, obtaining their skills has been dependent upon exclusivity. There are fewer than 200 medical schools in the United States. For entering students, their grade point averages, test scores, and their recommendations for entry are extremely important. Less than 2% of all applicants are accepted to licensed institutions. When you couple the exclusive nature of medical schools to the cost, you can see why so few people enter the profession. Total cost for medical school exceeds $375,000. We must also take into consideration the influence of the American Medical Association. They accredit medical schools which, in effect, lessens the number of teaching institutions. You can see why there are less than 650,000 practicing doctors in the United States. The number of American doctors relative to our population is one of the worst ratios in the developed world. But, and there is always a but, doctors in United States are highly paid. Their average income is 4.2 times the national average.

Besides doctors being in the top 1% of income earners, they are held in high esteem by the nation as a whole. It is a form of unrequited regard. Professionals, in this case medical doctors, are what we want our children to be. We do not ask our children to aspire to be janitors or maintenance engineers. We do not hope they grow up to be the garbage collectors or sanitary engineers. We hope and pray our children become doctors, lawyers and people of professional standing. It is not only the money. It is the respect and good will of the community we hope for our children. By giving doctors such recognition, they have leverage in the marketplace. They are role models to our children and guideposts for what adults should be. It is not a common practice for patients to negotiate a price with the doctor for his or her services. You do not go into a doctor's office and say, "Hey pal, I'll gave you $100 bucks to fix my broken arm." People do not even ask veterinarians what it cost to take care of their pets. There is an unspoken form of deference and respect doctors get because of their professional standing. I will suggest that many professionals take advantage of it. In general terms, there is no form of arbitrage for their services.

Another profession I would like to discuss is the legal profession. The same exclusionary process determines the number of licensed lawyers. I will suggest that because of the American Bar Association and state bar associations, we have arbitrarily high entrance requirements to law schools and this limits the number of lawyers.

Graduation requirements from law schools and bar examinations are a sophisticated form of exclusion. The lesser the number of lawyers, the greater the value in the marketplace. The supply of lawyers is determined by government agencies which are lobbied by legal associations. This practice creates situations where lawyers, in some cases in California or New York, can make anywhere between $700 to a $1,000 per hour. In many parts of the United States, these higher rates may be the exception but they determine the overall average income of lawyers throughout the country. The average lawyer makes 2.7 times the national average income.

Lawyers, as well as doctors, are as valuable as what they can be replaced for. Government sanctioned restrictions created by medical and legal associations limit the number of lawyers and doctors. Again, this practice creates high incomes. This is antisocial. The exclusionary nature of medicine and the legal professions are, in fact, hurtful to middle income and poor people. High prices for medical and legal services are socially regressive. Society is complex and sophisticated. We need the services of professionals but it takes a greater portion of money from middle or lower income earners than that of wealthier people to receive the same services.

I can make the same case for veterinary doctors, dentists, and other professionals. All of these professions limit the number of people with specialized skills. Their fees are high. Let me now discuss how emulation takes root in the professional class. Again, there are alternative facts. The big lie! Professionals perceive themselves as much more than workers. In reality, professional are just very skilled workers. They are the upper end of the working class. In actuality, limiting the numbers of people with specific skills is tantamount to unionization. Professionals are no more than unionized workers. Please understand they are workers and not some exulted class.

But, again I use the word but, professionals think they are in the class of the rich.

Most of their monetary earnings from their practices go into investment. They engage in the equity market, stocks, and the debt market, bonds. And, also in the real estate market. Their practices are secondary or ancillary to investment. They use their practices as money machines to fund what is most important to them, MONEY. Practicing medicine is no longer the profession of helping people. It is a profession to make large sums of money for investment. The same can be said about the law. The problem is the professional is only wealthy in comparison to the people below them. No matter how large their investments are, professionals are not in the same financial realm as the rich. They are no more than skilled workers. What differentiates them from the rich is the rich do not have to work.

If the surgeon loses use of his hands, what is he worth? If the trial lawyer loses his voice, what is he worth? Professionals perceive themselves as investors first. If they lose their ability to work, even with elevated incomes, they are as vulnerable as the people below them. The professional emulates like all other stratum. They think they are rich. The problem is they are only a heartbeat away from losing everything. They do not control the markets they invest in as do the uber rich. They follow markets. They are not market makers. They placed their monies in something that is bigger than them.

All of the social strata, except for the rich, have one major thing in common- they must work! Every other stratum, except for

the rich, emulates to deal with the insecurity
of not having complete economic autonomy.
The vast majority of people's socioeconomic
activities are counterproductive to their
security! They do not understand the
realistic values of their skills. They all think
they are something they are not. And, to
protect themselves, they close the doors of
opportunity to people below them. They
actually think they are higher up on the
occupational ladder than is the real case. Even
when someone initially makes it big. The
financial home run, they run into the trap of
irrational exuberance. They spend money as
if it will come in on a regular long-term
basis. This is not statistically the case. They
spend above their income streams as soon
there is an inkling of success.

They trade in their Toyota for a BMW
or Jaguar at the first sign that their income
levels will go up. They start to live the high
life and live large. They purchase above their
means. They are in an untenable position.
They start to believe the big lies of mobility.
They act as if the streets are paved with gold
for anyone who is willing to work long and
hard. Mobility and opportunity are no more
than the deceitful lies most Americans buy
into, even the professionals. Moving up the
economic ladder is difficult in a zero-sum
game. In actuality, the only group that is
protected are the rich. What protects them is
their vast accumulations of wealth. Their net
economic value. People below the rich are
cannibalistic in their desires to move up the
ladder. They are also cruel and unusual to
people below them by cutting off any lanes of
opportunity. Bigotry, sexual discrimination,
homophobia, and religious intolerance are all

manifestations of emulating the rich.

Everyone protects what they think they have the right to be. In truth, the chances of cracking the ceiling above them is almost nonexistent. The dreams we hold dear, the dreams of happiness, success, and certainty, are based on alternative facts or lies. Our folklore that talks about our heritage of equity and opportunity, for the most part, is baseless. Look at the last 25 years in America. Wages for the middle class have been stagnate. The number of the poor have increased greatly. But, and there is always a but, the rich have accumulated greater sums of wealth both absolutely and relatively to the other Americans. There were times during our history when there were greater levels of mobility and opportunity but that has evaporated into dreams. The 500 wealthiest Americans have as much net economic value and net worth as the bottom 50% of Americans. Five hundred people possess as much wealth as the bottom 150,000,000 people in our country. That is a fact! And, the accumulation of wealth for the rich is increasing at a faster rate than it is for the bottom 50% of the population. The gap is getting bigger. Today there is limited mobility. That is a fact! Each passing moment, mobility and opportunity becomes less and less. We are playing in a zero-sum socioeconomic game and we are losing.

Alternative Facts #7

The rich, what can I say. They are rich! Let me define them as people with a net worth of $1 billion or more. The number $1 billion is arbitrary but usually accepted as the measuring stick for the highest social stratum in America. Worldwide, there are between 2,800 to 3,000 people who fit into that category. In the United States there are over 1,200 billionaires. America has the largest number of wealthy people in the world. There is another arbitrary definition. Some people feel that having a net worth of $500 million brings you into the rarefied air of being rich. Estimates are there are more than 100,000 people that fit into this definition in America. In any event, these people are rich compared to the 7 billion people who inhabit the Earth. Now, take into consideration that dollars are worth multiple of dollars in a financial sense. This is the nature of leveraging, borrowing. The rich have money. More importantly, they have political and social control. In simple terms, they are connected. Being rich is the ultimate. It is the good old boys club. Money begets money. Power begets power. A good example of a rich person is Bill Gates. He is one of the wealthiest people in the world. Estimates are he has $70 billion of accumulated worth. It is not just his money. It is his political and social influence as well. His definition of how computers operate and what information is at our access determines our welfare, livelihoods, and societal structure. It is not just his money that makes him influential but also the structure of the world his computer operating system allows us to view. The information we gather makes him powerful because we see the world the way he wants us to see it. We see the world through his is lens. He is not a bad person because he is rich. Gates is a good person with good social intentions. He is the most charitable person in the world. He has given away billions of dollars for important causes. It is his economic activities that cause pain and suffering for others. I will contend that philanthropy is wonderful! It has saved millions of people from death, pestilence, pain, suffering and the indignities of life. But, there is always a but - philanthropy does not make up for the injustices of the marketplace. As I said before, we all try to promote our own self interests. Bill Gates just does it better than anyone on Earth.

The Koch brothers, the largest political donors to the conservative cause, leverage the money they make from the fossil fuel industry. They literally buy and sell political candidates on the right. Their influence in the Republican Party is legendary. For all intent and purpose, they direct the Republican Party and the Christian right. Money buys favor and political power. It is not an overstatement to say Gates and the Koch brothers use their money to advocate for their vision of society. They have the resource to try to inflict their will upon every person on the face of the Earth.

Even though the average person never comes in contact with the rich, they are who we emulate. Robber Barons like the Morgans, Rockefellers, and the Carnegies were held in high esteem. They were the founders of our industrial complex. Their transgressions of taking advantage of people and monopolizing markets are overlooked because they laid the roots of our industrial revolution. They are canonized in a non-religious way. Howard Hughes became a mega star in his own right. His every movement, his every action, was seen as that of a movie star to be held in the highest of respect. His eccentricities were viewed as odd but acceptable. If we acted the same way, we might have been institutionalized. Rich people are treated differently. The new rich, people like Mark Zuckerberg or Elon Musk, are held in God-like reverence. They are the guideposts of the millennium generation. The rich are more public than ever. This adds to their power.

People desire to emulate them. Some of the rich try to be viewed as ordinary but do not buy into the big lie as they are not. They determine our social mores and the paradigms we live by. They do it by the people they control. The very people we look up to they own. The people they use as conduits to the masses I will call "surrogates." The rich own and control people that are visible to us, their surrogates. We look up to them. We view these people in the media. Either the terrestrial media or the cyber world of social media.

People like Rupert Murdoch have an inordinate control over worldwide media. The seven largest media corporations control 85% of the information that we ingest. Pure and simple, big media disseminate alternative truths. They influence people for their own gain. The sell information for profit not truth. Their brand of truth is determined by its salability. It is entertainment not bent on actual facts. In many cases, media moguls

like Murdoch want to control our lives. His
brand of truth is no more than an
obfuscation of reality. He and his people
make up or massage the truth to create a
world to meet their public needs. They create
a vision of stability and certainty that we need
to feel safe. The vision is smoke and mirrors
with emulation as its reflection. Media
outlets through their depiction of the news,
motion pictures or non-documentary
programming set the social tenor for how we
live our lives. For the most part, our vision
for society is created by the media. The
news outlets where 85% to 90% of us get
our information help us make social decisions.
It is obvious that the news has been co-opted
by personal agendas of media ownership as
well as profitability over truth. Our sources of
information are not based on truths but on
political agenda or profitability or power.
News is spun to such an extent it loses its
credibility.

Alternative facts, or lies, are created
to enrich the few holders of wealth in
America. People buy into alternative facts
because they come out the mouths of people
representing the rich. The rich are portrayed
as mystical and god-like. We hear the names
Warren Buffett or Mark Zuckerberg or people
of the same elk and are enamored by their
every word. We do not take into consideration
how they monopolize markets to obtain their
wealth or the evils that monopoly throws upon
us. We do not understand how their picture of
what society should be being contrary to our
well-being. When we hear names like Mark
Cuban our ears perk up. Our eyes widen and
peel back. We see him on television and we
are transfixed. Many people are obsessed by

his opinions and ownership of a professional basketball team. They are not aware of his media connections or his influence in the marketplace. He is our hero because he speaks to truth. We do not realize it is his truth, not ours. He lives by an alternative set of values. The rich are no more than masters, lords, and kings because we let them be. We hold them in exalted positions. We give them power and sit at their feet. Remember Lord Acton's famous quote about power – that power tends to corrupt and absolute power corrupts absolutely. We are obsessed with the rich and envious of their position. They are the pinnacle of our society. There is a quality of godliness about them. They have been chosen. They are special. The term visionary or they look around corners as if we do not, is misleading. They just make more money than us. That is all there is to it. They are not better - they are just wealthier. We should not give them full reign to control our lives because we envy them. Their ability to make money should not prompt us to hold them in high esteem.

The phenomena of the new rich being in the public eye are a recent phenomenon. But, there is always a but – it is not their faces, it is what they own and what they do with it that influences our everyday lives. It is the power of their surrogates that influence us because we do not interface with them. They, even people like Mark Cuban, are isolated. They live in gated communities with bodyguards. They have spokespeople. As I said, we do not interface with them but their wealth buys power that controls us. They have control over our constitutional rights. Their politicians control our courts. They try to control our earnings and our customs and traditions. This occurs when we abdicate our power by emulating them and not protecting ourselves. The rich control and employ three major types of surrogate activities. Number one, the entertainer or the athlete. Number two, the politician. Number three, the church. Tied into the surrogates are the media outlets that distribute messages from the rich. We look to their surrogates for guidance. We hold their values to be sacrosanct or inviolable. These three groups of people, more than any other, determine our social rights and wrongs. They set the standards by which we live. The problem is that they are controlled by the rich to solidify and enhance their position of power.

The first surrogate we will view are the athletes. We, and our children, look up to them! If the truth be told, they are no more than gladiators in the historical sense. To watch them is like watching the slaughters that took place in the Roman Coliseum. They are chattels to the rich. But, they are leaders and role models for us and our children. Just ask Charles Barkley. They are no more than red meat to be thrown to the lions for the enjoyment of the rich. These gladiators are people that our children emulate and look up to. They give us values of competitiveness, discipline, and sacrifice. In reality, they are no more than slaves who entertain and make money for the wealthy. They are a rich person's crumbs that fall off their plates. We covet and hold them as national treasures. In truth, they are pieces of flesh.

Athletes are held in high regard as if being able to throw a baseball, or hit a driver 350 yards, or run 100 meters in less than 10 seconds is important. We feel that athletic feats are epic accomplishments in our society. The stature of Michael Jordan is imprinted upon every child in America. We still wear his jerseys. What he did on the basketball court is the making of folklore. Today he is more than 50 years old and we still hold him dear for what is no more than playing with a ball. We spend hours viewing an athlete's accomplishments. Memorializing what they have done or what we think they will do. We tell our children to be like Mike - Michael Jordan. Or, to be like Tom Brady. In reality, Michael Jordan and Tom Brady are wealthy beyond our comprehension. They are at the low end of the rich. They are one of the few slaves to be allowed in the 'good ol' boys club.' Thousands of other athletes toil for the folly of the rich and are no more than physical workers.

As I have said, the athlete is well paid. Professional baseball players can make $3 million-$5 million a year, as is the case with professional football and basketball players. That amount of money is many multiples of what the average American makes. However, their careers are short-lived. The average athlete retention of wealth is almost nonexistent. Over 50% of the players in the National Basketball Association, for all intent and purpose, are poor after five years of retirement. The Shaquille O'Neal's, the Magic Johnson's, the Peyton Manning's, and Alex Rodriguez's are the exception, not the rule, for managing money and fame. But, again I will put a caveat into our discussion.

Alternative Facts #7A

I am going to use Shaquille O'Neal as an example of the wealthy class. His net worth is estimated to be approximately $650 million. He is by all accounts now a committed family man. He is engaged in community projects to help the poor and disadvantaged. His interaction with children in the community is legendary. He is very philanthropic. Mr. O'Neill is progressive in his desire to help African-Americans. He is a good guy whose community service is applaudable! He is also wealthy beyond most people's comprehension. He has one of the highest Q ratings, name recognition, in the world. I will use him as a young African-American man who has actualized the dream of becoming an NBA star. It is important to note he did not forsake his education for his athletic career. Even though he left Louisiana State University early to play professional basketball, he continued his education. He received a PhD in criminal justice after his professional basketball career ended. He is well educated, maybe not extremely articulate, but he is mindful of other people. He knows where he came from. The values of family from his mother and his military stepfather were passed down to their son. Again, he is a good person, one you would be proud to have as a son.

Let me give you an example of how he can affect others unknowingly in a negative scenario. Be mindful, Shaq has a history of never hurting anyone on an individual or societal level. Shaq is what I call a gentle giant. He is, in fact, a glandular freak. In college and most of his professional basketball career he weighed between 300 to 310 pounds with 5 to 6% body fat. With his large frame of over 7'1" tall he, in essence, was a massive muscle. He dominated the sport for over a decade. Now, in his later years, he is almost 50. He is larger. He might weigh as much as 400 pounds. His body fat looks to be 18 to 20%. By any measurement, he is bigger than life. The example I will present is simplistic. It will be a metaphor for how one person can unknowingly affect the community around him. On a warm day Shaq decided to take his family to a local swimming pool. He brings all of his six children. Shaq walks over to the side of the pool and says, "Let me show you how to cannonball. Let's see who can make the biggest splash." He takes three gigantic strides and leaps into the pool cannonball fashion. With a huge splash, his massive body enters the water. Almost all of the water spills over the side of the swimming pool. Leaving an almost empty vessel holding little water. He gets up. He is knee deep in the near empty pool. He has cleaned out the pool! His simple action of having fun and playing with his children has taken away the rest of the family's ability to use the pool as it has been drained of water. There is not enough water left for his children to dive into the pool. They would get hurt!

Hopefully, you get the picture. Shaquille O'Neal did not want to affect his kids negatively. He did not even think about it. All he did was just jump in to have a little fun. This is the essence of a big player living large. Shaq is a good parent. He is a good person. But, and there is always a but - Shaq can't act in a laissez-faire fashion and only do what he wants to without recognizing it can affect others. He cannot put himself first. Using this same analogy in a marketplace is apt. Capitalists trying to make as much money as they can have the potentiality of negatively affecting other people in the pool. The bigger players seeking their own self-interests is for the most part a zero-sum game.

In capitalism when the big players attain profit maximization it is great for them. But, this system can't feed, house, or employee all of the other members of society! Capitalism does not distribute income in an equitable fashion. It never has and it never will. In metaphorical terms, the kids do not have a functioning pool to swim in when the big guy's profit seeking interests comes first. Shaquille O'Neil is a good person. He loves his children. He loves society. But the system, unfettered capitalism, must be regulated. Shaquille O'Neil cannot only think of himself. He cannot be allowed to cannonball. Rich people are not bad people. Capitalists are not bad people. By reflecting only on their self-interests, they do not understand how their actions affect others. You need a governor to micromanage how players in the marketplace act. You cannot let people like Shaquille O'Neil, the rich, make all of their own decisions. You cannot allow individual micro acts in the marketplace to create a macro system that is not advantageous to all of its players. The consequences of an "Us vs. Them" economic system is simple. It is a zero-sum game where the rich get richer at the expense of the middle class and the poor.

Alternative Facts #7B

A little bit more about Shaquille O'Neal. I said earlier a person is worth what they can be replaced for. At 7"1" inches tall and 310 pounds with great athletic ability and a high basketball IQ, Shaquille O'Neal dominated the National Basketball Association for more than a decade. He led the Los Angeles Lakers to multiple world titles. He was irreplaceable! There was no other center in the league that could match his skills, size, and ability during his tenure as a professional basketball player. He was the dominate player in the NBA. He earned over $25 million a year on the hardwood courts. Add to that an equal amount as a spokesperson for products and causes and as an entertainer. How can a person make that much money? It is simple! There is a great demand for watching, listening, or reading about professional basketball. This demand created tremendous revenues for the owners of the teams. It made great sums of money for the media outlets like ESPN. Money can also be made on legal and illegal gambling relative to basketball games and Shaq's individual performance. There is a social media presence for the sport and individuals in it. Money can be made there and the game has become monetized. Every time you see a game in person there are costs: tickets, food, parking, merchandise. If you see a game on TV or listen to it on radio, there are advertising or sponsorship costs. There are local and national television and radio licensing costs and revenues. Basketball magazines or newspaper articles or blogs where people follow the sport are monetized. All of these forms of demand for the sport and Shaquille O'Neal in particular costs someone something. It is important to note that Shaquille O'Neal gets a piece of all of the revenue. His salary, merchandising, guest appearances, and speaking engagements are all revenue producing activities. He is paid handsomely for his skills. His ideas on basketball, and even non-related matters, have a following. All in all, Shaquille O'Neal is in demand.

Let us compare him to us. How much money would someone pay to see you play basketball? How many articles or blogs or segments on television related to you would people want to see? Do you or I do anything that stimulates demand for our services? The answer is no. We are, for the most part, not salable. Shaq's demand is worldwide. Ours might not be outside of our circle of family and friends. The world market is gigantic. If you buy a <u>Los Angeles Times</u> newspaper to read an article that features a story about Shaquille O'Neal, his exploits have been monetized. Would anyone want to read about you? This monetization of Shaquille O'Neal trickles down to the size of his salary and numbers of his endorsements. If everyone in America is willing to spend one penny to either see, read, or listen to information about Shaquille O'Neal, that is over 300 million pennies. That is $3 million. Is he worth one penny to you? How many people in the world follow him? There are probably hundreds of millions outside of the United States that know and follow him. People are willing to spend money on magazines, going to games, or reading newspapers that have anything to do with Shaquille O'Neal. Relative to us and our skill sets, how many people are interested in what we do? Millions, thousands, or hundreds? The vastness of the size of the demand determines our value. The demand for anything related to Shaquille O'Neal generates revenue! For us, not so much! He has an enormous value. We do not! He is rich. We are not!

The same analysis can be used for people like Bill Gates. His operating system for computers has influenced our lives and the way we view the world. Warren Buffett's financial acumen or Elon Musk's visions are monetized on a global basis. They create immeasurable value for other people. Once acumen, visions, or skills are monetized it creates great value for that individual. This is how wealth is made. The very rich are few in number. They cannot be easily replaced.

Alternative Facts #8

As I said earlier, emulation is based on alternative facts and out and out falsehoods. People for the most part are not economically mobile, and opportunities are not easily available. Opportunities are more mystical than factual. Everyone protects people above them at the expense of advancing their own position. If you take this as true, this is disheartening at best and depressing at worst. Our dreams will never be realized and the alternative world we live in puts us at a structural disadvantage. Emulation puts us in a position where we may not be able to overcome our stations in life. We are not as static as untouchables in India but the streets of gold in our folklore are too far a distance to capture. The overlords, the people we emulate, are the masters of our fate by allowing us the few crumbs that fall off their plates. The problem is, if we buy into the big lie, we become appreciative of and happy for the little that we receive from them.

Our pittance in relative terms to the rest of the world is large. It gives us the wealthiest poor class in the world. The United States has the largest middle class in the world. But, there is always a but - in absolute terms relative to the rich the distribution of wealth and political power in America is one of the worst in the developed world.

On an individual basis our denial of our position in society relative to the wealthy puts us in a position of subjugation. There is a fix! All hope is not lost! In truth, we can rebel. We can receive our due. We are worth what we can be replaced for. We can increase our value with one simple stroke. All we have to do is become more skillful.

More salable! This is a simplistic notion, but it is doable. As with most important alternatives that change our lives, suggestions expressed in words roll easily off the tongue. In reality, change is a hard road to follow. Change is predicated upon discipline and sacrifice. These are characteristics most people find abhorrent. Let me personalize what I am trying to get to by an example. No matter what one's socioeconomic strata is - poor, unskilled, skilled, businessperson, or professional - we are all defending people above us. We emulate them and hold them in high regard. Just stop it! It is counterproductive to revere someone whose actions will be harmful to your well-being. Understand who the people above you are. Understand what they are and how they affect society.

Let us look at the class I called rich. They are not altruistic enough to bring about any meaningful change in society without benefiting themselves. If you are not mindful and do not recognize the goals of the rich are different than yours, you will be forced to forgo economic and social advancement. Remember the rich are not bad people they just have a different agenda. Their self-interest is different than yours. Self-evaluate! Pull back from what you think you deserve and live by what you are worth. If your skills render, you are worth $15 an hour or $30,000 a year. Do not act like the big shot. Do not spend more than you can afford to feel better. Do not portray yourself as more important than who you really are. If you want more don't rely on the eleemosynary proclivities of the rich to get it. Charity or philanthropy does not clear the playing field. On a social note, do not discriminate upon others because that validates their right to discriminate upon you. Do not think you are better than someone else based on social custom or old hatreds. Understand you are different, and differences are a sign of societal strength. There is a scale of social evaluation or order. Simply put, it is based on being at the top, being average, or being at the bottom.

We all know what the bottom is. It is defined and exemplified by people that we abhor. People we are threatened by. People that we want to extricate from our society because they frighten us. They are the dregs of the earth. We do not compromise in our disdain or hate for them. They are lazy, dangerous, oversexed, don't follow our social values or faith. They are of the wrong color or gender. They fall into many categories, but we know who they are. In truth, we do not like them because they compete with us for resources. Remember, it is a zero-sum game. It is simple - we hate them because they can take from us. An historical example is the American Indian. The old adage, "the only good Indian is a dead Indian," seems archaic. It is antiquated and, at best, shows how ill-informed our historical past has been. But, it's not just the past. There is still remembrance of yesterday. Go to New Mexico. Go to Oklahoma. Go to Indian reservations throughout the country. See how Indians live and how they are treated. It is no mistake that they are at the bottom of our social ladder. It is no mistake they die at a younger age. It is no mistake that their rates of diabetes and other major diseases are so high. It is no mistake that for the most part they are not well educated. Look at what we have and continue to do to them and their culture.

Just look at the slaves of yesterday brought to America from Africa. How much have blacks relative to whites progressed? Their political and social power is almost nonexistent relative to their numbers. They are demonized and hated. When they pressure for greater equity or restoration for past deeds they are dismissed. An example would be Black Lives Matter. Today it is not politically correct to overtly discuss their plight in terms of being inferior but many whites and Christians believe that to be the case. Our view of blacks is similar to our view of American Indians. It is racist and misguided!

Let us look at another group that we perceive to be at the bottom of our socioeconomic order - the LGBT community. Some of the greatest alternative facts have been used against them. It starts with biblical interpretations. Look at the Christian Right's feeling towards gays. Gays are disparaged and discriminated upon. They are classified as unacceptable members of our community. In some cases, Christian surrogates in Africa ask for the death penalty for practicing gays. There is a present-day hatred and resentment not founded on scientific fact. 6% to 7% of all mammals are bisexual. Being homosexual is not an aberration. Hating gays is an historical discrimination based in fear created by religious intolerance.

These three groups; American Indians, blacks, and the gay community are all held in contempt by the majority of Americans. They are not considered to be our equal. The people at the bottom have few supporters who think they have an equal place in society. These are but a few examples of disenfranchised groups. They are the bottom! I argue they are not unequal to us. In reality, they are only different than us. Ill-informed people vilify and subjugate these peoples to the worst of human biases. It makes racists and homophobes feel better about themselves. To some degree we all discriminate to feel better about ourselves. By identifying the bottom as abhorrent, it separates us from them and puts us at a higher social standing.

Now let us look at us. We are on middle ground. There are people below us. There are people above us. Below us they are hated. Above us there are exalted. The problem is, being in the middle is reprehensible because we are taught we are special. That is what emulation does. It is a way of filling an emotional insecurity. If you hate what is below you it lends greater credence in over valuing yourself. We pull up the false importance of the rich and push down our hatred towards the poor. We do this by feeling superior to the people below us and reverent to the people above us. We think we are special to bolster our hold over the poor. We hope we will be special like the admired rich who we emulate. In real terms, special means non-replaceable. Remember, you are as valuable as what you can be replaced for. By emulating you think you are increase your social value. That is a lie! It is easier to lie to yourself than to be disciplined and sacrifice to create a greater skill level. We will do anything that is cheap to make us more special. The problem is people do not accept a realistic evaluation of themselves. They wound others to have a better self-worth.

Here is an example. You meet a woman or a man that you feel attracted to. You get the courage to call him or her and make a social date. Because we are emotionally insecure we feel we want to make a good impression. We have all been there! You buy a new outfit. You get your hair cut or your nails done. You clean up your car. You fix up! You now drive over to your date's house and ring the doorbell. Your date opens the door. He or she looks at you from head to toe. They stare deep into your eyes and say, "You look nice not great, but you dress up well." You know that you date thinks you only look average. He or she continues, "thank you for the effort of cleaning up and trying to impress me." As the night progresses, he or she expresses you have average intelligence, no more, no less. Well, your date has burst your bubble. You know for a fact on a social scale you are above average.

Average is mediocre. You are not mediocre. You are special even though you have not put the effort into being special other than the superficial clean up. You want acceptance for free. You have been insulted when someone evaluated you at a lower level than you expect. You expect people to see you not as who you are but as who you hope to be. The problem is, it takes time and effort to actually be better than average. Emulating alternative truths are easier. Reality is hurtful.

Now is the last social group, the rich. We emulate them. We worship them. We build them up to be more than they are. They are not better than us. They are just different than us. The difference is simple. Because they have greater skills or different attributes, they are harder to replace in monetary terms. They make more money than us. They receive more affirmation than us. They out compete us in making money. They are not better than us. They are not more intelligent than us. They are only more differentiated than us in the field of making money. It is easier to emulate them than become one of them. To be like them takes discipline and sacrifice. Making money does not equate to being smart. All it says is you can make money. The good part about emulating the rich and placing them higher up the social scale is the higher up they go, the better we feel. We can feel better about ourselves for free if we emulate them.

The difference between the top and the bottom is now greater. Simply put, if the average is increased because the top is greater, and we are above the average, then our social standing is greater. The people at the bottom are further down. If the poor are pushed down and the rich are pulled up, we adjust ourselves to a higher stratum. It makes us feel better even though it is not founded on reality. It is no more than a house of cards. We lie to ourselves. We falsely feel we are more similar to the rich than the poor. The big lie is we think we are special. The big lie is if we are exclusionary it is rational and necessary. The real truth is there are only marginal differences between people. It is alternative facts that force us to push other people down to make ourselves feel more important. This is counterproductive. Emulation and the total disregard for the truth is at the core of our society. It is not healthy to live a lie. If we see more clearly society will change. The simple solution is do not buy into emulation. Ferret out the truth about yourself. In reality, we are no better than the people we hate that are below us. To exclude them in actuality is to exclude oneself. We are no better than others. We are only different. To look at our supposed differences and think we are special is counterproductive. It only helps people above us who we hold in high regard not because they are better but because they have money. Emulation is an effortless way to be like them. It is easier to dream of being great and wealthy than working for it.

In summation, increase your value by the training and education. It is imperative to continually do so. Do not live by feeling better by excluding, discriminating against, or showing biased against people you believe to be lesser than you. Do not accept the rich as God-like. Do not emulate other people. Accept who you are. Be proud of what you do. Do something about your failings other than taking it out on others. It is not easy, but you have to create your own mobility and increase your replacement costs. Do not live in the shadows of someone else. Do not buy into other people's claims of the easy way to better yourself. Look at Donald Trump and Mike Pence. They call their movement a populist movement. They say they represent the common person. They do not! They do not know anything about you. Look at the people around them. It should be evident and disconcerting because their very essence is counter to who you are. People like them, the rich and their surrogates are self-righteous. They exemplify the big lie. They have made it at your expense. They have created a zero-sum world and have gotten us to buy into the fact that it is reasonable for them to have so much and we so little.

Let me give you an example. I will be using Vice President Pence as a case in point. This exclusionary tale will be exaggerated but the pedagogy of over playing the example will create clarity. This example will drive home Pence's hypocritical deceit and hatred for people he feels are lesser beings. A hatred the rich and powerful have for people below them. Vice President Pence's daughter, Charlotte, comes home to his official residence at number 1 Observation Circle in Washington D.C. She tells her parents she is in love. "Daddy, I am in love with a great person. He has some flaws but who doesn't? He has been divorced. That shouldn't be a problem because President Trump has been married three times." Charlotte is building a case to gain her father's support. She continues, "Believe it or not he is even more recognized than you. And you are the Vice President of the United States! He is successful and considered to be the best person in the world in his chosen profession. And, Daddy, he is worth more than $500 million. He is a good Christian but not as active in the church as we are. I think you will love him. So will Mom." Mike Pence puffs up with pride. "Okay, who is he? Do I know him?" She smiles, "You don't know him yet, but you have certainly heard of him! You see him on TV all the time." She waits for a second." He should be here any minute. I have invited him over to the house." Within 10 minutes, a Secret Service agent walks into the Vice President's house. He announces to Pence that LeBron James is at the door. He is waiting to see Pence's daughter. Pence has little time to figure out what to do or what to say. He is frozen in fear that his daughter has fallen in love with a black man. With tattoos no less. He thinks he and his faith had taught Charlotte better. What is she trying to prove? Why is she so rebellious? When LeBron James comes into the house, Pence is respectful and courteous. The young couple leaves. The Vice President immediately looks for his wife. A dilemma of epic proportion. The Christian couple looks at each other and he ask, "What have we done wrong for our daughter to bring this person into our home. Into our lives?"

When Charlotte comes home, the Pence's have a talk with her. They explain to her that LeBron James is just not good enough for their little daughter. He is divorced. He is too tall. He has self-mutilated his bodies with ink. What kind of person would do such thing? She is heartbroken, but she will acquiesce to her parents' wishes. Their rationale was, "He is nice but not suited for you. Do you want to live in the public eye because of his fame?" They say anything to obfuscate the truth. It is pure discrimination and bias towards a person they feel is less of stature because of his color. Charlotte begrudgingly accepts her father's dictates because of her respect for him and his faith. Notice I did not mention his wife, Karen, because of the lesser role she plays in the household because she is a woman. The example continues. Charlotte says, "Okay Mommy, okay Daddy, I'll find someone new." In a couple of months, the broken-hearted daughter of the Pence's starts dating again. She falls in love. This time she comes home with the famous singer Marc Anthony who had previously been married to Jennifer

Lopez. The Pence's again tell the daughter he is not suited for her. They again present a host of reasons and a rationale for why her relationship will not work. In truth, Mark is Anthony is a Latino. That is not good enough for the Pences. Charlotte listens to her parents and breaks up with Mr. Anthony. She says she will find a more acceptable suitor. The next person she brings home is Asian. The same result! Her parents are not satisfied. Lie after lie, obfuscation after obfuscation. They keep telling their daughter the same thing. He is not good enough for you.

Charlotte decides to give it one more chance. Over time she will opens up her heart to a more elderly, mature white person. It is important for her parents to be more accepting. She finds a person more of her parents' generation. She brings home Martina Navratilova. This example is evidence of what her parents will say. They will not say no because Martina Navratilova is a homosexual. They will come up with some other rationale. What about grandchildren?

Black people, Latinos, Asians, people of the homosexual persuasion, they are all similar. To Mike and Karen Pence they are inferior! Their hateful attitudes, based on what they consider to be faith, is no more than the extension of exclusion predicated upon alternative facts and truths. In reality, no one is inferior. They are just different. It is disgusting and sickening that Mike and Karen Pence are making themselves feel better at the expense of others. They perpetuate a great lie to enhance their own feelings of superiority. Emulation satisfies us at the expense of others. It creates a false security. As I said earlier, it is a house of cards played from the very top of society down to the bottom.

Alternative Facts #9

Now let me present another concept that affects how we view truth. Information is the avenue on which we navigate our lives. It enlightens us and gives us direction. There is so much information it is hard to hone it down into intelligent bites so we can understand our environment. We must whittle it down to digest it. In Steffan Linder's book, <u>The Hurried Leisure Class</u>, he poses interesting questions. Does the speed of information have an effect on how we assimilate it? If information is King, do we view it in absolute or relative terms? How do we know if the King is telling the truth? Is what we hear factual and based on the scientific method or is it alternative facts to push an agenda? What roles do individuals play in accumulating the truth to make decisions? I will put much of Linder's thinking into my own reference points to show that information or truth is dynamic. Truth depends upon science not hearsay or folklore. What was held to be true yesterday is not always a given today. Remember we seek truth to fill the holes of uncertainty or insecurity.

I will begin our journey by looking at the Pilgrims who brought their beliefs and cultures to our shores. A good place to start is by reading the 1926 classic, <u>Religion and the Rise of Capitalism</u> by R.H. Tawney. To the Pilgrims, religion was king. They were not integrated people. They had little else but their religion. Most of their doctrines were predicated upon religious concepts developed during the Protestant Reformation. People in the 1600s were fundamentally following the teachings of Luther. Religious truth was the template for survival in the harsh conditions of early colonial America. People came to America for religious freedom and the opportunity of a new life. They live by what I will call the Puritan ethic. Hard work and parsimony were the basis of their existence.

Godly endeavors were paramount. People viewed going to heaven as being more important than their actual survival on earth. People relied on worship. They were driven by the opportunity of going to heaven. The afterlife was more important than their harsh present. If they did the right things, God would look down on them with favor. The truth of their origin and their existence came from the printed word in the Bible. God's teachings shepherded people through the tribulations of colonial life. There was little, or no, surplus of time because of the hardships that befell the colonialist. People had no time for leisure or the accumulation of treasure. It literally took 24 hours of back breaking work to survive. Any ability to consume less than a person's total production for a day's work was a chance occurrence. There was no margin for error and it took 100% of a day's work to survive. There was no rainy-day fund for the uncertainties of tomorrow. As I said, time stood still because people needed 100% of their efforts to survive.

Economic and societal growth were at a standstill. Information and truth were at a standstill. The Bible held all acceptable visions for a person's life here on Earth.

From the 1620's to the early 1800's time in America moved slowly. There was little social or economic progress. For the most part, the 1800's were the beginning of technological advancement and with it the furtherance of knowledge. We became more efficient in farming which lead to more free time. Manifest Destiny brought with it millions of acres of new land into production. This, in turn, brought about economies of scale. We got bigger. Excess time and treasure now allowed for investment in agriculture and manufacturing. Time needed for survival lessened and more time for the accumulation of treasure occurred. It did not take 24 hours of work to survive. It took less.

This excess time equated to new investment and knowledge. During this period, the church's teachings did not change. But, and there is always a but - the rate of economic activity increased and the accumulated growth of wealth started to accelerate. The old teachings of the church based on a static world were still sacrosanct. The church still vilified treasure in any form. It vilified capricious spending and anything that differentiated its parishioners one from another. The church was opposed to intellectual growth or social deviation. It viewed change as being demonic. People were held in check by the truths and values of yesterday. An example would be the witch hunts in New England in the 17th and 18th centuries. There was a time lag between reality and faith. The Bible was an instrument of yesterday's thinking. This was the beginning of alternative facts or truths in our everyday lives. The paradigms that guided our lives, the truths, where not in concert with the realities of our existence. We did not need 24 hours a day to survive. People now had leisure and the ability to create excesses. Facts relative to science and technology did not fit into the Puritan Ethic. Idle time was seen as the devil's time.

During this period there was real advancement in science. Because of extra time and treasure social interactions followed suit. The world was now dynamic. It was no longer static. The teachings of yesteryear were incongruous with reality. Leisure and treasure were unacceptable to the righteous. Science was unacceptable to the righteous. The righteous, or people of faith, were out of step. We started to accumulate capital, both technical and intellectual, which gave us greater advancements in production. Ergo, more extra time. We were more productive because of science. Christian religious doctrine did not accept any form of growth or science. They did not accept idle time. The Bible was not a living or dynamic instrument. As I said earlier, it was not in concert with reality. Facts that ruled our real-world experiences were at odds with our religious beliefs. A contradiction was growing in America. Religious people could no longer cope with the reality. They reacted by getting more deeply involved in the church. Conservatives react by going to the past. They do not grow. They do not progress. The church was based on outdated stultified faith where as the marketplace and technology were growing. Science was starting to take hold for the upper class. Faith for the poor. Science and knowledge for the rich. This divergence between science and faith caused a major clash between facts and alternative truths. I will contend that this is happening again today.

The next phase in American history is that of the Robber Baron. Capitalists harnessed the work ethic of the employee. By coupling advanced capital with labor, they increased production many folds. In doing so, the capitalists reaped the vast majority of rewards. People who had a solid work ethic in many cases were not skillful enough to adapt to the machines they were tethered to. A divergence. A new reality. A necessity for new truths. The Puritan ethic would have to change. Hard work had translated to getting into heaven. You could work hard but now you had to have skills. You had little market value unless you adapted to technology. What was the value of a work ethic if it could not be mechanized? With increased technology, many workers now had less value. As it were, less pieces of gold to show go your value. How could you get to heaven? With the advent of the Industrial Revolution and greater production from fewer employees, the entrepreneurial class received most of the gain from increase production. More gold, they were closer to heaven. At the same time, we were starting to see institutional unemployment and under employment. This was the beginning of a pool of little used or unemployable faith-based people.

Capital value increased and wages were stagnant. Look at <u>Capital in the Twenty First Century</u> by Thomas Piketty. Does this scenario sound familiar? Many workers are still subjugated to the truths of the past. They work just as hard in a Godly manner but received no greater benefit from production that comes with new technology and capital formation as was the case in former years. All or most of the excess that came from greater efficiencies that went to the entrepreneurial class is still the case today. There are new real-world truths to now live by. Wealth gets you closer to God. Workers are still encumbered by the Puritan ethic. The worker, in many cases, still works hard to get to heaven. They still live an austere life and work long hours. They still saved for a rainy day by foregoing leisure or consumption. But, they continue to fall behind the capitalist class.

The rich started to covet leisure and science and technology in the 1800's. They cast away traditional forms of humility and were no longer God fearing. They could buy God's favor. The real truth was capital increase production and therefore a higher living standard for the people that owned it. People like the Rockefeller's, the Morgan's, and the Carnegie's became the new guidepost for the nation. The new order in reality pushed aside the Puritan ethic and diminished the roll of faith in society. Money started to have a competing place with faith. People with wealth started to live a leisurely ostentatious life in plain sight of the workers who were stagnate. God gave way to the capitalist. Money not the Bible would determine facts and truths. The problem was the masses, the workers, still adhered to the old paradigms of life because little had changed for them. They started to accept they were different because they could not make as much money as the capitalist. The rich were growing in both monetary and intellectual terms. The workers did not. They remained stagnant. The workers were at a total disadvantage to the Robber Barons. The worst part was they bought into the idea they were inferior to people who made more money. They wanted to be like them. This was the birth of present-day emulation.

Let me fast-forward 100 years to the 1950's. The worker, the beast of burden, the heart and soul of America, had progress little in the ensuing 100 years. Hard working and God-fearing people's lives were essentially the same as their forefathers. There was little or no advancement in social or economic terms for the workers. Even their unionization, the advent of the AFL-CIO only marginally increased their standards of living. By now the real power in society was the rich capitalist class. It was no longer the church. The wealthy coveted money not the pages of the Bible that demanded conformity and humility. Let us reflect back on how much the average American actually changed. Between the colonialists coming to America and the 1950's, how much better off were the average Americans? How much bigger were their homes? How much better were their diet? How many more of their children lived? How much more educated were they?

In every category you would say they were better off. But, and there is always a but - how much better off were they relative to the entrepreneurial class? We did not even have a large middle class before World War II. It is my contention the workers' relative gains were small. There was little change in the workers lives until the 1950's. The average worker's gains were no more than the crumbs falling from the plates of the rich.

Exclusion had not changed very much from colonial days to the 1950's. The same groups of people were still discriminated upon. The discrimination was not as overt - it was more sophisticated. It was still there and it ran deep. Slaves brought over from Africa were still at the bottom of our socioeconomic scale. Indians, the indigenous people who inhabited America before the British came over, were no longer hunted but they were segregated to reservations. Women, even though it took hundreds of years to get the right to vote, were still second-class citizens. The Italians, the Irish, Catholics and the Jews were still discriminated upon. The disenfranchised workers still held vestiges of the Puritan ethic. They were still religious. But, to no avail. The real truth was they had a lesser or limited impact economically and politically. There were two truths people lived by. One, the rich lived by their own set of rules. It was exemplified by ostentatious capricious spending and power mongering. The second set of rules the non-rich still lived by was the old God fearing, Puritan ethic. Relative to the rich, the poor were becoming more powerless every day.

Something was starting to happen in the end of the 1950's. Hard-working people who saved money for a rainy day were finding out that their lives were not changing. They were still single dimensional as far a religion was concerned. Very little else was important to them.

The huge disparities in income between the owners of capital and the workers was getting larger. The rules, or laws or paradigms the average citizen live by, were counterproductive to their ability to compete with people above them. Savings were no longer important because they were too meager to make a difference. People holding capital and technology saw their earnings grow at an exponential rate. Worker's incomes were almost static. That is the case today. Look at the average wage relative to inflation the last 30 years. There were no measurable gains for the average worker whereas the top 1% of wealth holders saw their incomes increase at rate of 16% per year. The reliance on the Bible and the teachings of God were starting to lose their relevance in the 1950's. There was a need for new truths, but religious people were late coming to the table of change. The vast majority of them were inert. Well educated people, as there is a correlation between wealth and education, advanced with science and technology. Poor people who are less educated and religious were more static. As an aside, this is an argument for continuing free education not privatizing education as many conservatives' advocate.

Now let me again fast-forward to the 1960's. Because of the Vietnam War, Keynesian economics, and federal deficit spending we moved into a period of institutional inflation. Not only would prices increase but the quality of goods and services would worsen. Technology and market forces would create obsolescence. Things began to move fast. Anticipatory inflation was causal in speeding up consumption. Worker's skills were not keeping pace with capital. Most poorly educated people were living on past alternative truths. They were still buying into the big lie. They thought they were more than they were. This new emulation was being pushed by advertising and marketing. Because of greater production, new products were brought to market at accelerated rates. The workers were still taught that savings would show God their humility and get them into heaven. These teachings were pervasive at the same time society was facing inflationary pressures. Money in effect started to have less value. If you did not spend your savings or money today its purchasing power decreased. Savings lost its allure.

You could no longer say to God, "Here are my savings. Here is the proof of me being humble and hardworking enough to enter your house," when the value of your work was decreasing. Why save if the value of money you hold decreases? Old truths or facts told us to save for a rainy day. Show God you could sacrifice and be compliant with Christian humility. This was now counterproductive. People had to readjust. They could no longer stay true to the old Puritan ethic.

They slowly lost their vision of going to heaven. Live by working hard, humility and savings would lose its luster. The problem was these values were no longer consistent with a faster paced life where you had to spend your money before it lost its value. The workers looked at the lives of the rich. They now wanted more than simple religion. They became more integrated. Since they did not have to save, they now had more money for leisure and consumption. Workers started to covet the values of the rich. They would see a greater need to emulate the rich because they now viewed the rich as Godly. The new leisure of spending money to maximize its value started to creep down to the worker! Many people asked themselves where is the truth? Do I work hard? Do I live a humble life? Do I save money? Or, do I live by today's realities and direct my life toward consumption I can't afford? Am I trapped by the truths of yesterday where everything was stagnate or do I live the big lie of emulating? Other questions came up. Is spending money more important than making money? Is hedonism more important than humility and Christian religious beliefs? How about my 15 minutes of fame? The big question. Is money more important than God?

Alternative Facts #10

Let me present another example of how people do counterproductive things to their social and economic well-being. I will preface my remarks by saying that technology, science, and breaking from archaic religious doctrines set people on a new path of reality. People from the 20th century to the present have what I call accelerated incomes.

Rising incomes create greater propensities for consumption at the expense of savings. Because of inflation money saved loses its value. People must consume faster to fend off the marginalization of money due to higher future prices. People spend more at an accelerated rate to escape from the ravages of anticipatory inflation.

Here is an example that will show how alternative fact or truths do not mesh with the reality of inflationary pressures. We will look at an upper-class income professional, Jake. He makes $150,000 - $200,000 a year. He works at Silicon Beach. Money is important but so is the prestige of being in the .com world. No longer does a one income household make enough money to provide the goods and services that young professionals deem necessary. Jake must find a person of his financial equal as a life partner. He can no longer marry down as was the case generations earlier. She, in this case, is Sammy, also a professional in the .com industry. They make similar salaries. The couple spends every penny of their incomes. She totes a Valentino purse, she wears a Vince or Burberry blouse, James Perse pants, and of course Louboutin shoes. To further her power position, she drives an E350 Mercedes convertible. Jake similarly fits his half of the power couple by driving a Range Rover. He wears Rag and Bone jeans, a Hugo Boss shirt, the Kanye West edition of Adidas tennis shoes and, of course, a Submariner Rolex watch. Jake and Sammy are all fluff and no substance when it comes to savings. They live for the moment. If they do not spend it now their money will lose its value. They cannot just let it sit there.

Let us throw leisure into the equation. Remember, if you are static, money loses its value. In many cases, it loses its value at an accelerated rate. To offset this, you must be hyperkinetic in your spending. Jack and Sammy can never stand still. That is not just in financial terms. Hyper drive leaks into the social and emotional parts of relatively young, affluent people's lives. Here's an example. Neither Jake nor Sammy can stand in line at Starbucks without looking at their phones. Their iPhones are the lifelines to their existence. So is anything that has to with communication or online entertainment.

Today Jake decides to do something physical. He is going golfing. It is one of many activities he has scheduled for the day. Remember, just hanging out is counterproductive to the value of your earnings. Jake never walks the golf course. It is imperative that he takes a cart. Six hours on the links will shorten the rest of his day's ability to spend money. Life for him is always one more thing! He is always partaking in one more activity as if the world is ending tomorrow. If you are on the golf course too long, you do not have time to maximize your economic effort.

Let us look at another endeavor. For many upwardly mobile people cooking is the rage. Culinary skills are now augmented by technology to save time. The electric knife, a convection oven, microwave, and even the delivery of pre-ordered food to prepare for yourself. It takes too long to shop. Let someone else do it. It only will cost us money of a declining value so let us augment cooking to get it done faster. Anything that will afford Jake and Sammy a quicker meal and greater chance to spend their money is acceptable. Culinary skills, the art of preparing a great feast for oneself and others, is now time sensitive. You have to do it fast to have time to spend more of your money.

Another example. The essence of hyperkinetic living is taking the car instead of being peripatetic to cover a short distance. To allocate time to walk from point A to point B when it is more scenic, healthier, better for the environment is cast aside because of time sensitivities. If you walk for an hour, there is less time to spend your money. Of course, this can be offset by bringing your phone and buying things online. Besides being hurried, people augment their time with technology. Technology creates greater efficiency which allows you more time to maximize the value of your money. You spend money in the near term, not the long-term. It has greater value in the near term! Let us go from walking to assimilating information. Most people get their information by viewing it rather than reading it. It simply takes more time to read than it does to watch. Therefore, people learn about the world and their place in it by watching TV, Facebook, Twitter or YouTube on some type of device. Sitting at home reading a book does not maximize your ability to spend your money. People become spenders not thinkers. By viewing the world on a device, you are a spectator. By reading, you are a participant. Participatory endeavors take time. Because of that, they are cast aside. It is easier to read a summary than a treatise. Everything we do is hurried! Just one more thing. By being hyperkinetic, we limit our ability to have a true read on our environment or our way of life. People read books less each generation. If you are a reader, you read summaries. Viewing takes less time than reading. Remember the importance of time and using it efficiently! Everything you do is hurried. Everything you do is predicated upon spending as much of your money as possible. To fully understand something and appreciate its value it takes time. Time is the last thing that Jake and Sammy want to waste. Time is money.

Let me give you another example. I ask you, the reader, to come with me. I suggest we go camping in a remote part of the Rocky Mountains. Some beautiful place in Colorado, God's country. There are a couple of provisions. Simple ones. No phone or electronics. No technology. Not even books in this example. How long would you last with only personal interaction and your own thoughts? When was the last time you were alone? Truly alone without augmenting your time with either material things or another person? When was the last time you did not have material things to play with or mindless technology to bide your time? When was the last time you reflected on your belly button, navel gazing or *omphaloskepsis*? I am going to suggest there is a reason you feel uncomfortable in the slow setting of thought and reflection. You feel uncomfortable and anxious because you are not maximizing the value of your time. Remember time is money. You want to be able to spend more of the decreasing value of your money. This might not be a cognitive thought, but it is the essence of your being. Hyperkinetic activity is driven by the almighty dollar.

Now, what is the logical extension of all this? The most time intensive thing you can do is think. And in the world we live in today, that is the antithesis of our lifestyles. People do not think they quickly wade their way through information to react. They get their information to make the smallest or the biggest decisions of their life in the quickest most time efficient manner. They buy into alternative facts and truths that are easily obtainable and socially acceptable because to think or probe is too time-consuming, People want what is the lowest hanging fruit no matter if it is true or not. Truth has no place when expedience is all that matters. People do not think. You and I want facts based on cheap conspiracy theories, urban legends, and alternative facts. We accept intellectual dishonesty. We live by anything that is mindless. Anything that takes the least amount of time to assimilate is our *Ocums Rasor*. Life is hurried, it is not directed by truths. Alternative truths are easy. They are not provable but who cares. Alternative facts fill up our insecurities. They drive us to maximize the value of our money in our hurried leisurely lives. Who cares where we are going as long as we can spend your hard-earned treasure. People do not care about what is real based on scientific proof. People only care about spending and pretending to be something they are not because spending money fills up our insecurities! Do not think it over, just react! The same analogy for time and money can be made for time and social and political truth. Just react, do not think is not acceptable. In dealing with the problem of alternative facts, we must be deliberatively thorough and act promptly in replying to lies.

Science over faith, fact over fiction, the greater good for all verses the selfish needs of one or a few is the only way our democracy will survive.

Alternative Facts #11 SUMMARY

There are reasons why people make up alternative facts. There is reason for intellectual dishonesty. The reasoning is based on insecurities and perceived threats. John Jost, an academic from New York University, feels that cognitive thinking of conservatives and liberals are quite different. Conservatism is associated with epistemic order. The need for safety is built into their genes. Order, structure, certainty, constancy, simplicity, and familiarity are all hallmarks of conservative people. Conservatives have extensive concern about personal danger. They have extreme anxiety and sensitivity to threats and imminent death. That is their DNA makeup. Liberals are more concerned with new experiences and seeking happiness in the future. For them, life is constantly changing with hopes of betterments in the future. Conservatives are more static whereas liberals are more fluid. Conservatives feel change is a threat whereas liberals feel it is an opportunity. It is arguable that conservatives are emotionally happier. They, for the most part, lead more fulfilled lives. They find their center and stick to it through the facts they assimilate that describe their environment. Most conservatives feel that they, and only they, should have the right to determine or protect their destiny.

Liberals feel the same way but are not as strident. It is evident that the threat of uncertainty and death is more powerful than looking for future rewards. Conservatives are afraid of existential forces because that would portend a lack of control. Liberals feel that environmental forces are beyond their control. They should align themselves with change.

In our complex and sophisticated world, truths are moving fast. It is virtually impossible to assimilate the information that is being created on a daily basis. Liberals embrace this change as positive. Life is an adventure. They are drawn to progress even if it means changing the principles they live by. It is built in their genes. Their DNA is different than that of a conservative. Liberals are progressive and forward thinkers. Their glass is half-full. Future events will fill up the other half. Conservatives, on the other hand, are wired differently. The view change as a threat. They feel the dangers of progress. To protect themselves they respond negatively to anything that is new. They react to anything that threatens the nature of their belief systems. They are called reactionaries. It is neither good nor bad, but liberals are progressive. They seek constant change.

Each group is taking in facts to validate their view of the world. Facts do not have to be real, all they have to do is fit into pre-existing social, emotional, and political paradigms. People love what corresponds with their existing schema. Anything that is contrary to their perceived notions of right or wrong is seen as a threat.

People are seeking veracity to validate how they live their lives. Anything is acceptable. Conspiracy theories, lies, twisting or embellishing facts, exposing false equivalencies, and denying science are the tools of validating one's existence. Both conservatives and liberals will accept any or all forms of alternative facts if they help defend their values. You would hope that truth would get in the way of preconceived notions however, most often, it does not. Bigotry, hate, and lies to protect one's ideology are usually more powerful than the truth. This must change.

Liberals fantasize about what could be. Looking into the future to find what it holds is not as strong an emotion as protecting what one already has. The strong belief of defending one's social, emotional, or physical being is a trademark of conservatives. They are more fixated in their beliefs than liberals who aspire to fulfill their dreams. Beliefs in alternative truths are more important to conservatives than liberals. It does not mean what they are doing is wrong! It just means what they are doing is different than liberals. Their thinking is different in content and emphasis. By the very nature of their genetic makeup, conservatives are frightened and inert. Liberals are dreamers and more progressive. They believe in the advancement of ideas. They are optimistic and fluid. Conservatives do not want the world to change. Their beliefs are more closely tied to yesterday's reality. Their counterpart, liberals, as I have said, are dreamers. They view change as inevitable and fortuitous. Liberals may accept alternative truths, but they are less tied to them. It is a matter of emphasis. Dreams can dissipate and may not always be clear. When something, a dream, is fleeting it is hard to defend. A liberal's DNA makeup accepts compromise. They are willing to gamble to have a better future. Theirs is not a bird in the hand philosophy.

As I have said before, people are wired differently. Conservatives and liberals have different DNA or genetic makeups. It could be their environment or it could be by birth, but people do not see things the same way. In any event, people are insecure and grab at straws to fill the voids of uncertainty. As information and knowledge increase, people are inundated with more facts than they can assimilate. People become more uncertain and unsure of their position in society with too many choices. In many cases, uncertainty causes liberal thinkers to seek more adventure. Uncertainty causes conservatives to bunker down in the past.

The dynamics of different people exposed to the same facts seeking different outcomes is exacerbated by emulation and hurried leisure. There are many reasons for alternative truths or facts. We need clarity. We need to see facts derived from the scientific method through an objective lens. We must fight against our proclivities to want to make ourselves feel safe. We must view the world as it is and not always look to tomorrow. Our need for personal order causes the need for alternative facts. By seeking order, we often view others as being of lesser stature. Looking down on others gives greater purpose to who we think we are. This is dangerous and exclusive. With the advent of science and technology, viewing more information than we can assimilate creates new rules to live by. We must take into consideration how conservatives and liberals are wired. They view similar events in dissimilar ways. The fight for limited resources are not just rich versus poor. It can be expressed as black vs. white, male vs. female, homosexual vs. heterosexual. All countervailing groups want to project their position upon others. We must make sure that their positions are based on provable facts. To reach a maximum value as a citizenry and a maximum value on a personal level we must rethink what is important to us. We must view things in objective, not subjective, ways that are not driven by insecurity and uncertainty. Different opinions or views must be seen as giving us a larger aggregate of information to compromise with. True facts create clarity and can only hold if we purge ourselves of preconceived notions.

Alternative Facts #12

Elizabeth Warren's book, <u>This Fight is Our Fight: The Battle to Save the Middle Class</u>, was written in 2017. It is a tale of how America has moved from the New Deal ideology of inclusion developed by Roosevelt to an economy predicated upon exclusion. This has taken place with the advent of conservative ideas from Ronald Reagan to the present. Warren discusses how the New Deal was responsible for the development of America's middle class. The New Deal stabilized the economy by creating effective demand. Most historians present the New Deal in two components. The first New Deal, 1933 to 1934, and the second New Deal, 1935 to 1938. The first iteration of Roosevelt's plan to revitalize the economy was written into law in his first 100 days in office. It was highlighted by the following legislations: The Federal Emergency Relief Administration, the Civil Works Administration (CWA), the Security Acts of 1933, and the National Recovery Administration. The passage of these bills helped to stabilize the banking and financial sectors of the economy and created jobs. The second New Deal included the Wagner Act, Works Progress Administration (WPA), the Civilian Conservation Corps (CCC), Social Security, the United States Housing Authority, the Farm Security Act, and the Fair Labor Standards Act of 1938. These pieces of legislation allowed workers to unionize, created jobs, and established the pension system. They dealt with the agricultural sector, housing problems and established a minimum wage.

The first and second New Deals created what economists call effective demand. The depression lowered our GDP by almost 50% and caused massive unemployment. In effect, there was no demand for products although we still had the same ability to produce products. What was lacking was income to buy products. Roosevelt poured billions of dollars into the economy. The free market was not working. The government had to pump prime the economy.New Deal legislation plus World War II spent America out of the Great Depression. In the simplest terms, government spent large sums of money. It also regulated the economy to dampen down the swings of the business cycles. More importantly, the government created a situation that allowed for the growth of the middle class. With government help America would have a more equitable distribution of wealth. In Senator Warren's case, it allowed for her parents - her father was a maintenance worker - to enter the middle class. It allowed their daughter to get a law degree. With the help of government assistance, she became a lawyer. She later became a law professor at Harvard University. From there she took a government position in the Obama administration. She became a political force because of progressive regulation of the free market. Doors opened up for her and millions of Americans to move into the middle class. From a modest beginning she became one of the most powerful women in the United States. She is the essence of the American dream. Government regulations and subsidizing the promotion of the middle class afforded her the opportunities for social advancement.

In dealing with the devastation caused by the Great Depression, President Roosevelt and other liberal thinkers followed the teachings of John Maynard Keynes. His book, <u>The General Theory of Employment, Interest and Money</u>, written in 1936, is a classic. The Keynesian approach of government intervention into the marketplace led to the secession of the downturn of the economy and the beginning of the middle class.

From Roosevelt to President Ronald Reagan, economic growth averaged 4% to 5% a year with few major economic downturns. The problem for the wealthiest people in America was the more government regulation, the less accumulation of wealth to the top income earners. Keynesian regulation diverted most of the new growth in GDP to the middle class. It will be my contention that Ronald Reagan and Presidents Bush, Clinton, Bush, Obama, and Donald Trump all followed a conservative road map, which has done two major things. Number one, the greatest portion of the distribution of wealth is now back to the rich. From the 1980's to present, for all intent and purpose, wages have been stagnant whereas the top 1% of income earners have seen their incomes increase on an average of 15% to 16% year. Number two, a deceleration of growth in GDP to approximately 2% a year. With the new economic reality there has to be new alternative truths to allow for a new redistribution of lesser levels of wealth.

I maintain a whole industry has been created to develop new truths or alternative facts that the average person buys into which promotes the conservative agenda. Fox News is an example of such a media outlet. Their dissemination of falsehoods has enhanced the rich at the expense of people below them. Companies like Fox News spew out lies and alternative facts. They are part of a corporate and business structure that has created the most inequitable distribution of wealth since before the Great Depression. It started with the wealthy, individuals and corporations, co-opting the Republican Party. Now they co-opt both parties by the large sums of money they contribute to candidates at all levels of government. The new direction of American politics takes advantage of the middle class. It suppresses the poor. I will use a phrase I have used on numerous occasions, "in simple terms." The new political elites, whether they be Democrats or Republicans, are trying to undo the progress made by the New Deal. Both Democrats and Republicans are more corporate. They follow the dictates of big money.

The Democrats are slowly eroding the progress of the New Deal. Conservative Republicans are moving full speed ahead to eliminate it altogether. Even the mainstream of the Republican Party is trying to privatize Social Security. They are trying to end the minimum wage. They are against equal wages for women. They are trying to dismantle Medicare. And, they want to deregulate almost every facet of the American economy. They have tried in every way possible to strip the support, the safety net, from the poor of this nation.

Today there is little or no economic growth. The GDP is increasing at 1% to 2%. It is very much a zero-sum game. The top 1% of income earners in relative terms lost to the middle class from the 1930's to 1980's. They certainly have made up their losses from the 1980 to the present. Less government means more wealth for the rich. The new realities of the stagnant or declining middle-class precipitates the use of alternative truths. It is clear there will be fewer and fewer Elizabeth Warrens in our future. The opportunities she took advantage of because of New Deal Keynesian ideology are being stripped away by conservative policies. The wealthy want to reestablish the old guard and revert back to an economy as deregulated as our present-day economy, which led up to the Great Depression. One could argue that we have too many laws on the books that hamstring business. I maintain they are not enforced. They are window dressing. Buying into the big lies of what conservatives say is too much government which takes away opportunity. It is counterproductive to the middle class.

Alternative Facts #13

I want to discuss the economic relationships that led to the Great Depression and the New Deal. I will present some of the alternative truths that allow the average American to accept the regressive state of reality we are in today. I want to discuss the lies the middle class have accepted that have led to its slow decline. We have previously stated that emulation and a leisurely hurried way of life contribute to class distinction. I want to discuss how economic growth creates instability and insecurity that exacerbates the differences between classes. There is a need for alternative truths and alternative facts if the middle class and the poor are to accept their lower standards of living more easily.

With that being said let me lay out the theoretical constructs of a free enterprise model. The free market has caused the great distinction between classes. This model will represent the conservative philosophy that is pervasive in the Republican Party of today. As with all models, there are some assumptions: One, in the marketplace there are many buyers and sellers. Two, both the buyers and sellers are small and insignificant. Three, there is free entry and free exit into and from the market. Four, both the buyers and sellers are price takers. Five, the products sold in the marketplace are deemed to be homogeneous. Six, there is little government interference. The government provides internal and external defense. The government is the arbitrator of contracts. And, the government prints money to facilitate economic activity. The basic tenets of this model were developed by Adam

Smith in 1776 in <u>An Inquiry into the Nature and Causes of the Wealth of Nations</u>. The book's basic premise is that people promote their own self-interests in the marketplace. Their incomes are derived from the sale of what he called the factors of production, which are land, labor, capital, and the capitalist. The remunerations to these factors were rent, wages, interest rates, and profits. Wages are the remuneration for one's labor. Rents are payments for the usage of land. Interest rates are the payments for the usage of plants, equipment, and inventories.

Profits are the payments for entrepreneurial skills and risk-taking. In a laissez-faire market, people would sell the factors of production to generate income to live their lives. Monies are to be used to feed one's families or provide whatever consumption needs they desired.

People go into the marketplace and promote whatever maximize their abilities to generate an income. Everyone is self-promoting. In a competitive market, people are producing goods and services without any government regulation or interference. These products are produced for a profit. The products, in turn, satisfy the needs of the consumer. The consumer gains their income from the sales of the very factors of production that produce the products. Anything imaginable can be demanded or supplied in the marketplace. The market is driven by self-interests of receiving wages, rents, interest rates, or profits.

The market is also driven by the strings of self-interest for both the supplier and the consumer. Incomes allow people to demand any product we desire. Income is derived by the production of said goods and services. The marketplace is a self-promoting circuitous exercise. A product is produced to generate a profit by employing land, labor, and capital. This income in turn generates demand for products. The theory behind the supplier's products generating income which generates demand, is called *Say's Law*. John Baptiste Say developed this theory in 1803. It is the backbone of laissez-faire or conservative economic philosophy. What makes this theory beautiful is supply creates demand. The economy will function efficiently as long it is free of outside influences. Those influences, simply put, are government regulation and government interference. The profit motive tied with people seeking rents, wages and interest rates drive the economy to produce any products within the scope of science and technology. The economy will be efficient and promote full employment and price stability. As with all models, it was held to be perfect.

In reality, the model did not take into consideration business cycles or what lay people called uneven growth. Economies do not grow at a steady state. They grow in fits and starts. There are different phases of economic growth that are classified into one of four stages: prosperity, recession, depression, and expansion.

Say's Law presented itself in such a way that the only reason there were business cycles was because of government intrusion. If the government would opt out of any form of regulation, the economy would always get back to levels of full employment and price stability. This concept was called automatic restoration to equilibrium. The economy has the ability to grow to limits of its inputs.

The only limits are the amount of resources, people's ability to develop new technology, and the desire for people to want to self-promote. The economy is seen as a perpetual spinning top that is always in balance and is growing into its limits of knowable and useable resources. There is a mechanism for stability and equilibrium. It is called automatic restoration to equilibrium, which can be seen by viewing four variables: demand, wages, prices, and savings. Let me exemplify how the economy falls out of steady-state growth and returns to equilibrium. For some reason the demand for products drops. This only seen as a momentary slippage. But, and there is always a but - if demand drops, it will affect the other variables. Instantaneously, in a free market, if the demand drops wages will drop to offset the lower level of income that is received for the product. This sets off a chain of events. Instead of firing workers to compensate for any lost demand, worker's wages will go down. Wages are seen to be flexible. Demand goes down, wages go down and this will be offset by the prices of products going down. In a competitive marketplace there is flexibility. As these variables go down, the value of money saved will go up.

Let me offer an example. The price of an orange is a dollar. Wages are a dollar. When the demand for oranges drops it will be offset by wages dropping to $.50. Workers did not lose their job but they accepted lower wages. If a person had one dollar saved when prices were a dollar, they could buy one orange. Now that prices have dropped to $.50 savers have the ability to buy two oranges. In any flexible economy where people do not lose their jobs demand will be offset by lower wages. The value of savings goes up. This cycle of lower demand, lower wages, lower prices, and a higher value of savings can continue until the price of an orange reaches $.10. At some point, the extra value of savings will have gone up to such a degree that the saver will determine the price is low enough to purchase the product. That, in effect, has created a greater demand which will increase wages, increase prices, but the value of savings will start to diminish. As prices go up, the purchasing power of savings go down. People end up having the ability to buy fewer oranges. Therefore, they will spend their savings as quickly as possible to take advantage of this increase value. Prices will go back up to one dollar. Wages will go back to one dollar. The marketplace will be an equilibrium without a loss of employment. The only thing that has changed is savings. In the long-term, savings will build up again because of stability in the marketplace.

Conservative economists believe the marketplace is resilient. In the long run, there is always full employment and price stability. Let me summarize. Laissez-faire, or the competitive market, is based on self-interests. People seek wages, interest rates, rents, and profits. Say's Law states that supply creates demand. The final piece of the puzzle is automatic restoration to equilibrium, developed by Don Patinkin of the University of Chicago. The economy's equilibrium point is at full employment with stable prices. The competitive model is perfect as long as there is little interference from the government. This model was held to be the case until the Great Depression. Conservatives blamed the Great Depression on government interference. Liberals had to develop a new theory to show how the government could stabilize the economy and dampen the effects of business cycles. The aforementioned model was called perfect competition, free-market economics, or laissez-faire.

Starting in the 1930's, economists believed that the role of government had to be increased to regulate the market. We now use what is called the Keynesian model of imperfect competition. Free market economics is called perfect competition. It is also called supply-side economics. Imperfect competition, the Keynesian model, is called demand driven economics.

Alternative Facts #14

The next model I will present is called *imperfect competition*. It deals with oligopoly and monopoly. As usual, there are some simple assumptions. Number one, in the marketplace there are many buyers but only a few, or one, sellers. Number two, the buyers are small and insignificant whereas the sellers are large and significant. Number three, there is little or no entry into or exit from the marketplace. Number four, the buyer are price takers and the sellers are price setters. Number five, products are differentiated or there is no substitute. Number six, the role of government is large and forceful: the government provides internal and external defense.; the government is the final arbitrator of contracts; the government prints money; the government protects the worker from the owner; the government protects the poor from the rich; and the government protects the consumer from the producer.

In this model, the government plays a large role. It regulates the economy by regulating employment, GDP, and prices. Liberals view the marketplace as not being perfect. Therefore, a need for government intervention. The marketplace is only momentarily stable. It has business cycles that are not self-correcting. Prices are not always stable and full employment is illusionary. Liberals do not accept Say's Law of supply creating demand. They believe demand creates supply. Finally, liberals believe the economy will only reach an equilibrium through government intrusion. Equilibrium will not necessarily be at full employment nor prices be stable. Arbitrary governmental decision will determine economic activity. Conservatives, on the other hand, say economic activity is solely determined by the marketplace. Historically, the conservative model leads to a misdistribution of wealth and the protection of property rights. Conservatives believe in self-reliance. Liberals believe that with government intervention there will be a more equitable distribution of income. They champion the protections of civil rights. They believe in the "it takes a village" sharing concept of income distribution.

Liberals feel that government involvement in the economy is mandatory. Government's role is to adjust. The bigger the economy the greater need for government. Without being pedantic, I will discuss the concept of automatic restoration equilibrium again. This time with a liberal interpretation. There are four variables; demand, wages, prices, and savings. In the liberal model when demand drops, people will be fired. There is no flexibility in wages. Wages are held to be inflexible because of unions and minimum wages. Prices are not flexible because of oligopolies and monopolies. Because of the lack of competition leaves the economy with one or a few suppliers, prices are held to be sticky. When demand drops, there is no mechanism to restore equilibrium. Demand drops, and unemployment ensues. People must now use their savings to survive. Make note of the fact that in United States savings rates are extremely low - maybe 2% of net income. We run into a situation where there are not enough savings to be spent to bring the economy back to equilibrium. Thus, the necessity for government. The government must create what is called "effective demand". It will pump prime the economy back to higher levels of employment and consumption. To bring about effective demand, the government can use policies of raising or lowering taxes and spending more or less. This is called fiscal policy. The government can expand or contract the money supply thereby changing interest rates which is called monetary policy. Or, the government can spend in a deficit. These policies have the ability to create effective demand to drive economic activity. These policies are created to put money into the hands of the consumers and producers. With increases in demand because of government intervention, there will be increases in employment and investment. Wages will go up. The economy will expand. Prices will increase and we will see higher levels of equilibrium. This is called *demand side economics*.

The government will target equilibrium, employment, and the price levels. Government intervention into the market place will hopefully bring about GDP increases of 3% to 4% annually. Employment rates should stabilize at 95%. And, there will be targeted price increases of 2% to 3% as measured by the consumer price index, CPI.

Liberals feel the government must regulate the economy. It is inherently unstable without it. Conservatives feel the marketplace should be regulated by the promotion of self-interest. Conservatives feel we should get the government out of the business of regulation. There should be no unions or artificial wages. The economy should function in a laissez-faire manner. It will self-regulate itself to full employment and stable prices. Liberals feel the necessity of a large government. It is needed to cure the ills of imperfect competition. Liberals do not believe in the notion of automatic restoration to equilibrium. The two philosophies are at odds. As I said earlier, conservatives feel the marketplace is based on self-interest and the protection of property. If you are successful, it is predicated upon your own hard work. Remember, you only as valuable as what you can be replaced for. Conservatives feel that the cream will rise to the top and if you are not successful, it is your fault.

Conservative philosophy is personalized or individualized. If you are not successful, it is because of a lack of competitive skills. As I said before, if you fail it is your fault. Your safety net is your skill level. If that is not enough, then you can get help from your family. Next comes the church and then private philanthropy from others. Your success and survival are up to you and your ability to garnish resources from others. In simple terms we live in a world based on the survival of the fittest. If you fail, it is individualized and you are inferior. Do not forget, the marketplace is based on competition. Everyone has equal opportunities of failure or success.

Liberals, on the other hand, say we fail because of structural imperfections in the marketplace. Oligopoly and monopolies strip us of the chances of being successful. Remember the concept of a zero-sum game. In an imperfect market, the rich can take advantage of the poor. The owner takes advantage of the worker. And, the seller takes advantage of the consumer. These inequities should be addressed by the government. It is the government that is last line of defense against of exploitation. The government is the helper of last resort. If you fail in the liberal model, you can fall back on your family. If you need more assistance, you can fall back on the church. If that is not enough, then you can seek philanthropic aid. The last resort is you can take advantage of government transfer payments. The government will transfer monies from the most successful individuals to the least successful.

I have presented two distinctively different schools of thought. Conservatives feel if you fail it is your fault. Liberals feel if you fail it is systemic and the government should come to your aid. One model, the conservative model, is based on self-reliance and self-interest. The other model, the liberal model, is based on government interference. As I have said before, I am what is considered to be a bleeding-heart liberal. I relish the role of government as a protector of the poor, the worker, and the consumer. I think my taxes should go to help others. My tax dollars that go to other people are one of the prices of being a member of society. I think being part of society has social costs as described in Thomas Hobbes book, <u>Leviathan</u>, published in 1651. My conservative friends, on the other hand, are more interested in individualizing one's success or one's failure. They are more directed by Charles Darwin's concepts of survival of the fittest, <u>Origin of Species,</u> written in 1854. Conservatives feel they owe society and the other individuals in it nothing. Both positions, liberal and conservative, have historical clarity. Neither one is better than the other. But, and there is always a but - believing in, or following, one of the two major theories will take us on different paths.

One path is self-reliance. The other is government reliance. We need to have facts based on the scientific method to ferret out which of the two forms of government we as a society we want to follow. It is the facts and how they are delivered that will create our notion of right or wrong. Whoever controls the information we make decisions by are the winners. There are always differences of opinions. It is important that both sides protect their position with truths not alternative facts. For example, it is the news media's job to be the conduit of facts. It is not their job to solve problems or give opinions! The news should not be bias!

When we make individual choices, they should be based on facts that are provable, not opinions! It is our job to call out lies. It is our job to understand our opponents' agendas. Being contrary to someone else's opinion is acceptable. Note that we do have theories and facts at our disposal. They are everywhere. It is imperative that our theoretical constructs be based on science and provable facts.

Let me summarize what we have done. We have presented two competing economic theories. A competitive model that conservatives stand by and an imperfect model of competition that liberals stand by. In both cases, economic activity creates incomes which determines how we live. It is imperative that we understand the economic, social, and political paradigms we live by. For that purpose, we must have a knowledge

base predicated upon truths. If we are to
function as a democratic society, upholding
the truth is of paramount importance. We must
stop lies or alternative facts in their tracks.
The truth is immutable and it should be
viewed as such. Truth should override
personal agendas or opinions.

Alternative Facts #15

My last theory. Simon Kuznets' definitive work written in 1941, <u>National Income and Consumption"</u>, discusses the nature of business cycles. We previously mentioned the 4 phases of the business cycle: prosperity, recession, depression, and expansion. Kuznets discusses the causality of business cycles and how they play a part in the redistribution of wealth. He believed that, depending upon which phase of the cycle (wages, rents, or interest rates) was diminished at the expense of increasing profits. His general notion was business cycles were an inherent problem in pure competition. He showed statistical proof that the amplitude of the cycles would get larger and larger over time. The only solution in dampening the swings of the cycle was the introduction of government regulation. During different phases of the cycle, different economic groups gain over others. A zero-sum game.

Overall, he felt the majority of gains from business fluctuations would go to the capitalist or entrepreneurial class. Their gains would be greater in expansion and prosperity. Their losses would be less in recession and depression. Alternative facts would have to be created to mitigate the loss of income and wealth for the middle class and the poor. Kuznets was the father of econometrics, or mathematical modeling of economic activity. He surmised the larger the economy the greater number of transactions. Note: do not forget that laissez-faire is predicated on people seeking their own self-interest. The market was no more than millions of transactions of buyers and sellers to meet their selfish needs. The more transactions, the greater level of economic activity and, therefore, the greater level of national income. In his analysis of economic events between 1919 and 1938, he showed that the more transactions taking place in the marketplace the greater swings or amplitudes of the business cycle. He exemplified this by what was later called the *jumping bean theory.*

A transaction of a buyer or seller was equated to a jumping bean. Jumping beans are frijoles saltarines. They are inhabited by a small moth called cydia deshaisane. The bean jumps or moves when heat is applied to its surface. The moth is awakened to a state of activity. The beans will move in a random fashion. Kuznets envisioned the beans being in a vessel. The vessel was the marketplace. With the addition of more beans, more selling and buying transactions, the vessel would move in a random fashion. It would vacillate. The more transactions the more beans and this would cause a greater the level of movement. A greater amplitude of swing in the business cycle. With more beans in the vessel it would levitate off of a flat plain. It could either smash upward on the ceiling or drop to the floor and smash. In either case, there would be economic catastrophe. The upward swing, expansion and prosperity, would cause hyperinflation. In essence, overheating of the economy. The downward swing, recession and depression, would bring about massive levels of unemployment.

It was Kuznets' contention that the government would have to dampen the swings of the business cycle. It would have to hold the amplitude of the cycle in check by some form of regulation. Government would apply pressure on the vessel. Therefore, the swings of the cycle could not go too high or drop too low. The economy would be targeted for steady state growth. In simple terms, the regulatory force of government would have to be increased. This would stabilize the amplitudes of the business cycle. The government would use fiscal policy, monetary policy, and deficit spending to regulate the economy. Automatic restoration to equilibrium does not work in an imperfect marketplace. To stop hurtful swings in output, Kuznets felt there was a need for government intrusion. If the market was competitive, then automatic restoration theory would hold. Kuznets was one of the leaders of the Keynesian movement that held the competitive market model was based on false assumptions. False assumptions that lead to a false reality.

Alternative truths. We never had or will have a competitive market. The truth is, the market distributes wealth and income disproportionately in the favor of the rich. It is plagued by depression and hyperinflation. Look at the book, <u>Capital in the Twenty First Century,</u> written in 2013 by Thomas Piketty.

Kuznets maintained that the government involvement in regulating the economy was obligatory. It was the only way to create what he called steady-state growth. The laissez-faire free-market model was not stable. The capitalistic system of people pursuing their own interests had to be regulated. This new economic reality would be called a mixed economy. Today most economists accept this as a given. Government regulation of the economy is synonymous with the earth being round. It equates with the factual existence of global warming. The only debatable elements of the notion of a mixed economy is how much government regulation is necessary. And, in what sectors of the economy is it applicable. Private enterprise works exceedingly well if, and only if, there is a profit attached to the production of products. The problem is that not every economic need of the individual or community can be filled by the profit motive. Some necessary goods and services, social overhead, cannot be made for profit. Capitalism does not have the ability to feed, house, and give health care to all of the citizenry. There is no economy in the world were these basic needs for survival are fully provided without government regulation. Only government can produce goods and services that are needed for maximum social welfare. Food, shelter, medicine, education, roads, dams, defense, are all unprofitable endeavors. They cannot be privatized and distributed to all members of society. This is a fact. There are no real facts that dispel this truth.

One last notion. Joseph Schumpeter, in his book written in 1909, <u>Capitalism, Socialism, and Democracy,</u> discussed how technology and innovation affected business cycles. Innovation caused greater shift of resources to the rich. Therefore, a need for government regulation to equitably distribute wealth. The more innovation, the bigger swings in the business cycle and greater misdistribution of wealth. With greater inequities of wealth, Schumpeter felt that democratic decisions would be determined by a small number of people. Business cycles pushed by technology advance the economy. But, and there is always a but - this leads to more authoritarian political power for the rich. The advent of technology passed more power to the elite.

Now let us get back to our basic premise that facts and truths must be aligned with reality. The 1% of income earners who control over 50% of the wealth in the United States disagree the notion of a larger government. They oppose the notion of more government regulation and redistribution of wealth. They will lie to keep their wealth. They try to push as truth the Trickle-Down Theory of economics. They live by the Laissez Faire Theory of economics which does not exist. They express the evils of government whereas progressives applaud government. For that purpose, the propertied class have to create a sophisticated media industry to disseminate alternative facts. They control our politicians. They control our role models. They have a huge influence on the church. And, in many cases, they are accepted as God like beings. We, that is you and I, are at fault. We emulate. We lead a hurried leisured life. We seek the lowest forms of information to guide our lives. We accept lies over facts. Most of our social and economic activities are counter to our own welfare. We do not exert enough of our energies to be more valuable in a political or economic sense. We are passive when it comes to protecting ourselves. In reality, the insecurities and uncertainties caused by the market should be a call to arms. We should evaluate our plight and seize the moment. We need to push for a greater share of the bounty of economic activity. As I have said before, "words are cheap." Making changes are easier than you think! It all starts with

weeding out the lies and accepting the truth.
We must discourage alternative facts and seek
the truth. There is a need for greater
government involvement, not less!

Alternative Facts #15A

I am going to present an example that might be offensive to many of you. Our conservative leaning economy cannot and will not provide health care for all Americans. Conservative ideology dictates that health care must be driven by the private sector. No major nation in the world has been able to provide adequate health care for all of its citizenry without universal government coverage. Our mixed economy cannot support private health insurance without people falling into the cracks of no or minimal coverage. This is a fact! This is as true as the Earth is round, not flat. There are no provable facts to say otherwise. Every major country in the world that provides health care for all of its people do it under a government single-payer system.

With that being said, it is foolhardy not to push for universal health care in the United States. The conservatives have come up with a whole industry of alternative facts on why government mandated health care from single-payer to a highly subsidized form of private insurance will not work. The July, 2017 Congressional Budget Office's estimates of the Republican 2017 BCRA, or Better Care Reconciliation Act, forecasts that up to 25 million Americans will lose their private insurance in the next decade. It forecasts that insurance rates will increase by more than 100% in the next 10 years. These numbers, by and large, are indicative of private health care programs that Republicans have developed to replace the Affordable Care Act.

All of the alternative programs to

repeal and replace the Affordable Care Act, also known as Obama Care, are no more than tax savings programs for the rich which will ultimately excludes millions of Americans from health insurance. This is a fact! Even if the Congressional Budget Office estimates are off by a factor of two, it still means that 10,000,00 to 15,000,000 Americans will lose their health insurance. The fact of the matter is there is no place in the world where the private sector can house, feed, or give medical care to all of its population. No matter what the Republicans say, private sector medical attention is woefully lacking. For private insurance to be successful it would have to either raise rates so high that many Americans would not have access to get into the market. Or, whatever type of insurance that is provided will not provide proper coverage. For private insurance to work, younger, healthier people must be placed in a pool with older, less healthy people. Young people will pay higher premiums to take care of older people who are sick and cost more. That is how insurance works. The young and healthy are in the pool to pay for and offset the costs of the old and the sick. This is an actuarial fact! Profit seeking insurance companies cannot and will not enter markets that have uncertainty or are not profitable. The only way to provide health insurance is a single-payer program. But, and there is always a but – if, in fact, the Republican or conservative plan works, there will be insurance. The new policies will not have needed basic coverages. The policies will not provide for existing illnesses. There will be limits on the total amount of coverage. Many procedures will

not be covered without a special rider.
Pregnancies, ambulance services,
pharmaceuticals, and more will likely be left
off most policies. As I said, free enterprise
can't provide proper health care because
there's no place in the world where it has
been a profitable endeavor.

If the middle class and the poor buy
into the Republican plan that talks about
people having the ability to buy their own
plan, and if Medicaid fixes per capita caps, or
if the federal government blocks grants to the
states, they will find the market failing them.
Even if the Republican plan goes into effect,
the CBO suggest millions of people will either
not have proper coverage or no coverage at
all. The overriding question is why people are
accepting alternative facts which are harmful
to their health. There is no legitimate reason
to think that we can have a free enterprise
health care system for all Americans. What the
Republican Congress and Senate are proposing
in their health care act is unattainable! Again,
why do people buy into it? Some of it must be
people are so opposed to what has happened in
the past that they will accept any promises of
a better future. Some of it is their hatred for
the government. Some of it is their hatred for
liberal ideas. Some of it is that many people
trust their politicians on a major issue and feel
it will carry over to all issues.

Let me present an example. A voter is
unalterably opposed to abortion. He or she
thinks that abortion is tantamount to killing.
Abortion holds an important social or political
position in their consciousness. If a member
of the House of Representatives or a Senator
represents your position on the issue of
abortion, you accept his or her positions on all

issues. In this example, your right to life representative is also opposed to government mandates for health care. Your congressman is opposed to a single payer system, Medicaid, Medicare, or any restrictions upon private insurance companies and pharmaceutical companies. He or she holds the Republican Party position. The problem is, they are more interested in their own political careers and less interested your health. They have bought into the dictates of the American Medical Association, the pharmaceutical industry, the health insurance companies, and the far right's major donors such as the Koch brothers. Your congressperson's interest is ideological. They further his or her political stature not your health. Politicians spew talking points that are alternative facts. They obfuscate the truth about your health care. They lie! They do the bidding for special interests and the rich. In any event, the programs they advocate will take health insurance away from millions of Americans because they are based on privatizing health care. Some of the members of Congress or the Senate may actually be disdainful of people below them - the average American. These congress people are, in effect, only protecting the rights of the rich. Again, why do people believe them?

Let us get back to abortion. When people emphasize one position so strongly, abortion, it can blind their view of other issues. They are easily led astray. To embrace and follow a politician on one issue can leave the voter without proper alternatives on other issues. To protect oneself people must seek the truth. They cannot accept the low hanging political diatribe that is counterproductive to their well-being. The truth is out there. It is just harder to obtain than the cheap, vicious lies that permeate our media. How many people read the CBO's scores on health insurance? If you do not read it or investigate health insurance, you pay the price. In the case of national health insurance, your life could be at stake!

This example has been presented and is obviously directed toward the obfuscation of truth by conservatives or the Republicans. Later I will talk about welfare. I will discuss the alternative fact that liberals or progressives used to promote their position on protecting the poor and disenfranchised. The Democrats are no more truthful in discussing welfare than the conservatives are when they discuss health insurance. Liberals will downplay the cost of welfare programs. They will say it is cheaper to pay for things now rather than later. They will overplay the effectiveness of welfare. They will not discuss the fact that many people take advantage of welfare. There will not discussed that welfare is a self-perpetuating program. It traps generations of the poor and makes them wards of the state. They will not discuss the fact that welfare promotes the poorest to accept government care rather than become independent. Liberals will not discuss the fact that welfare subsidies are so great they can bring about a generation of women having more children than they can take care of. Liberals or progressives disseminate alternative facts as well as conservatives do. It is our job to call both of them out. We must seek the truth! Take note: liberal or Democrats protect civil rights. Conservatives protect property rights. In the above case, if the conservatives pass their health care legislation, the rich will win out. Lower taxes for top 1% of income earners - a 3.4% millionaires' tax. Do not buy into their false truths. When we talk about welfare again, I will warn you of the information the liberals present to pass welfare legislation. Both sides lie. Do not buy into it.

Alternative Facts #16

Before I direct our discussion to alternative truths, I must clarify my thoughts on how to gather information. In earlier chapters I have said that I am an old fool and that I am a bleeding-heart liberal. Now, I will tell you that I am not under any illusion that you, the reader, will endeavor in a scholarly approach to getting to the truth. Many of you do not have the time. Many of you do not have the inclination. Some of you do not care and, some of you do not have the access to real information. Taking this into consideration I will present an approach to look for real facts if you so desire.

I have offered up some theories that give us insight into why people accept or create alternative facts. I want you to realize I have simplified all hypothesis, assumptions, and theories I have presented. The theories are based upon published works. The theories were presented to understand the social paradigms and economic axioms we live by. I want the reader to be able to fact check what has been presented and to be presented the truth. I know for most Americans reading is harder than listening. It is harder to read a book in entirety than read a summary. It is easier to live by gossip or jokes on late night television than dig into the bowels of information. I want the reader to understand there is no correlation between truth and ease. Looking for the easy way to obtain information most often leads to misunderstandings or falsehoods. Seek truth! Act like the town crier. Call it out. Call out truth when faced with falsehoods. There is an adage, "speak truth to power." I am going to add a corollary – you cannot speak truth to power until you speak truth to yourself.

Let me try to create a path or vector we should follow to begin to educate ourselves as a citizenry. We must be informed enough to protect ourselves from others. As I have spoken earlier, people generally try to emulate and lead a hurried leisured life. The need to create certainty and stability is exacerbated by the vicissitudes of a changing economy and social constructs. In times of turbulence caused by increasing technology, reach outside of yourself. I am hopeful you will begin a voyage of being more informed by simply reading more. It is not just more. It is also the type of material you read. Seeking more fact-based information will broaden your interpretation of the world around you. If you do not read, then use your hand-held devices and listen or watch informational channels or websites. Seek out information based on the scientific method not conspiracy theories or folklore. If you are a person of faith, view the Bible or Koran or any religious document as a living document. The advent of new information and knowledge makes their interpretation time sensitive. The world is dynamic. Religious teachings must be viewed through a changing lens. Literal interpretation of religious documents should give way to the intent of the authors. Do not look at the letter of the Bible or Koran. Look for the intent of what the authors were trying to convey. It you are looking at science, recognize over time there is a new understanding of the truth. What was held to be the case yesterday must give way to the new realities of present day. New information and technology make the acceptance of new truths imperative. With knowledge there is light. The more knowledge you have the greater control you have over your environment.

I will use the word wisdom. Wisdom is the control over one's environment. That control can come from your experiences or you can digest someone else's experiences. Digesting someone else's experience can be in written form, exemplified by their actions, or passed down orally from one person to another. Any form of information that you absorb must be based on facts. When seeking clarification of past, present, and future ideas, they must be based on science. Facts are science driven. Faith must also be viewed as dynamic and comport with reality. Most importantly, facts can be replicated.

Let me present a list of books that are at the backbone of our Judea - Christian Eurocentric life. These books represent the core of ideas we purportedly live by in democratic nations:

The Bible
The Quran Muhammad,   609-632
  The Prince, Niccolo Machiavelli,1532
Leviathan, Thomas Hobbs,   1651
  Principles of Mathematics, Philosophiae Naturalis, Principia Mathematica, 1687, Sir Issac Newton
Origin of Species, Charles Darwin,1859
The Republic, Plato,   380 BC
An Inquire into the Nature and Causes of the Wealth of Nations, Adam Smith,
                              1776
Das Kapital, Karl Marx,   1867

<u>Theory of Relativity</u>, Albert Einstein,
1907
<u>The Magna Carta</u>,   **1215**
<u>The Constitution of the United States of America</u>,   **1789**
<u>William Shakespeare Complete Works</u>,
Shakespeare,   **1623**
<u>1984</u>, George Orwell,   **1949**
<u>Critique of Power and Judgement</u>,
Immanuel Kant,   **1790**
<u>An Essay Concerning Human Understanding</u>, John Locke,   **1889**
<u>Institutes of the Christian Religion</u>,
1536

Obviously, there are other books, but the reader should view these publications in a context. Use the following books as a framework to understand our economic, social, and political environment. Other important readings to put things into proper context are: <u>The Story of Philosophy</u>, written by Will Durant in 1926; <u>The History of Economic Thought</u> by J.B. Bell, written in 1976; and <u>The History of Political Thought</u>, written by Bruce Haddock in 2005. Remember, wisdom is the ability to control your environment. Wisdom is predicated on knowledge and knowledge is predicated on facts. There is no room for alternative truths!

Alternative Facts #16A

I want to add another personal observation. Most people will not read nor investigate anything that is remotely technical or sophisticated. I hope I have not passed that boundary. Most people have difficulty even listening to people of knowledge or authority. This is not so much because of their understanding of the issues but, rather, it is because people feel they are just as knowledgeable as authorities in any given field. For some reason the 24/7 news cycle, our constant need for information, our stimulus from smartphones, iPads or computers make a statement we are smart. Without proper training or the commensurate amount of time studying any discipline, we feel that we have acknowledge on any subject. We all feel our opinions are meaningful and hold weight. To be honest, this is not the case! We are familiar with more things than any time in our history. However, this does not translate into understanding things that are complicated or sophisticated. I think we all suffer from exaggerated self-worth when it comes to thinking we are informed or smart. We are not brain surgeons yet, if you watch *Grey's Anatomy* on television, you sure as hell think you are. We should take to heart Malcolm Gadwell's 2008 book, <u>Outliers: The Story of Success</u>. It presents a 10,000-hour rule for proficiency. We all think we are smart but one cannot be without putting in the hours!

Let me give you a situational example we all fall into. We must guard against our own over exuberance relative to our intellect if we are to seek the truth. My wife and I were out to dinner with some friends. We all wanted the night to be social, so we said we would not discuss either health issues or politics. Health issues at our age are depressing. Politics are always maddening. Well, you know what happened. Donald Trump's name came up. Someone at the table vilified him. Someone at the table went after the democrats as a countervailing argument to dispute President Trump's accomplishments. One side was speaking in generalities. The other side was speaking factually. The discussion between the two parties became contentious. Everyone at the table, except for the two combatants, were embarrassed. One of the two was quite vociferous. He was a wealthy investor with a net worth of $100 million dollars or more. He had an ego to match it. He felt his money made him smart. He wanted to be heard. He did not want no to listen to anyone! The other person was a world renowned academic. He is a very respected Dean at USC. He was little full of himself. Both men are good guys. The businessman was an avid Fox News junky. He only read conservative mainstream blogs like the *National Review, Real Clear Politics, Red State,* and *Dick Morrison.* He thought he stood intellectually toe to toe with the academic. He was convinced his positions were correct. He would not listen to the renowned authority because he felt his opinions had greater weight in the conversation. There was no compromise in the man. There was little give and take between the two men but the academic would at least listen to the businessman's position. He was trying to understand how someone could look at things so differently. Maybe there was something there? Both men's spouses finally interceded, and the political discussion stopped. Later that night the academic confided in me, "It was hard to open up to someone so closed minded."

As a bystander it was interesting. I have learned not to get into political discussions. It does not do any good. They are frustrating. No one listens! My training is such that I have read more than 1,000 books on interdisciplinary approaches to political and social problems. It took me a long while to understand that not many people care how knowledgeable I am or what I think. Most people are not open to my expertise. The idea that the businessman felt he was on the same intellectual playing field as a Middle East authority because he was highly successful and wealthy was alarming. He based his opinion on alternative truths and did not even know it. He actually felt he was correct in his position. The Dean never came down from his ivory tower. He was condescending. I am sure he was correct in his analysis but talking down to someone does not open them up to accepting a new point of view. The academic was patronizing to the businessman. He finally said,

"Why would you expect me to accept your knowledge on the bond market and not acknowledge the time and effort I have put in studying the Middle East? I would never question you on financial matters. It's your field! What makes you so arrogant to think that my life work is so easily refutable by someone who hasn't put much effort into studying the Muslim world? If you gave me some advice on purchasing some stocks or bonds or offered to work with me on some real estate deal I graciously appreciate your help. Why don't you respond to my expertise and listen to me and expand your horizons? Accept what I have to say! I can help you understand what's going on in Syria because this is what I do. I have studied the Middle East for over 20 years. I have been there on numerous occasions. And, I have personally met some of the principles on both sides of the Syrian conflict. I don't mean to be talking down to you, but you will never have a better source of information then me."

The investor's wife glanced at him in a fashion only a wife could. She was pleading with her husband not to argue anymore. He backed off from the argument and graciously said, "Why don't we just agree to disagree and leave it at that?" I give credit to both men. They left their feelings at the table and everyone got back to socializing.

I am sure you have been placed in a similar position. Both men are people of goodwill. Neither man was mean-spirited. They both truly believed in their positions. Neither one was willing to compromise. One was ill-informed and the other was condescending. There was no give or take! Here is what I got from the incident. People, no matter how well informed they are, should be able to communicate without talking down to other people. People, no matter how successful they are or wealthy they are, should understand what they do not know. People should be open to information. The truth is out there. It has to be packaged correctly. People have to be seeking it in a more sophisticated way. You have to throw out your ideology, your ethnicity or religion, your gender, your preconceived notions predicated upon your economic standing, and a host of other intellectual impediments if you desire the truth. Alternative facts or lies are a lazy person's way of trying to gain the wisdom to control the environment around you. Accepting cheap lies will give your environment advantage over you. Not the other way around. The upshot of all this is you must listen. You will have no control over your life if you are ill informed. Listen to a different voice than your own! Do not be arrogant because of your wealth or talk down to people because you are well educated. Compromise and seek the truth. Embrace it, share it, and live by it.

Alternative Facts #17

I am going to present a few examples on how both the conservative right and the progressive left are fooling themselves. I will talk about the importance of religion to the right. Then I will talk about the misdirected welfare state of the left. Let me discuss religion first.

There has to be a reason on an emotional level that lies are so acceptable. They augment emulation, uncertainty, instability, and a hurried leisurely life. For too many people, lies are a way of validating who they are. People abide by alternative truths - lies - as long as they get what they want. People like President Trump are promising something so primal with virtually no cost that millions of followers gobble it up. When I hear him lie, I am amazed people buy into what he is selling. But, they do. On July 23, 2017, the *New York Times* fact checked his first 180 days in office. He has lied in speeches or texts on an average of 5 times per public pronouncement. I have mentioned on numerous occasions that most people believe in things that are counterproductive to their own well-being. What people like Trump offer is like what drug peddlers offer to their clients.

Accepting alternative facts is a lazy and selfish way of dealing with reality. It is in line with social usage of drugs. The short run effects of accepting lies are like an out of body experience. You feel like you are in a world that is safe. A world where your problems will be addressed. It cannot be a substitute for normal life situations.

Lies are cheap to disseminate. There are major costs in accepting them. The long-run cost of ingesting the devil dust, lies, is always ruinous. Lies are hurtful. They do not protect you from the truth! They are addicting. Unfounded facts cause great damage to family, friends and society at large. For many Americans there are a short run freedom for not having to deal with reality. The long run cost of being addicted to alternative facts is that they encumber your future.

Let me present an example inside an example. You are a religious person. If you are, I probably have offended you! I am not asking you to be like me. I am agnostic. I am asking you to view the Bible in today's terms, not literally as it was written. The world has changed so much there is little historical relevance in the Bible or Koran. There might be spiritual or emotional importance, but that is subjective. We no longer live in small villages. We no longer are static in location and knowledge. We live longer with more material wealth.

Science has created a new landscape and all that is in it. We are not remotely the same people as when these two religious books were written. That is the case! The world has changed! I am asking you to take this into consideration. The clan mentality of exclusion is no longer applicable. We do not have to fight over land and food to survive. We are not in a state of war against the elements or other people to survive. We live in greater proximity to others. There are more of us. Everything has changed! If nothing else, we cannot be exclusive because technology has created a world that is predicated on connectivity - for machines as well as people.

We cannot view ourselves as distinctly different from others around us. Our DNA expresses that we are all humans. None better. None worse. We cannot literally learn from the deeds of the apostles because the world we live in is so much more complex. We cannot fight with clubs in a world with guns. Yesterday's literal interpretation of life is not applicable in our modern environment. We must view the teachings of the Bible as metaphors or guide posts of a moral code to live by. The code must grow with the complexity of society and the people in it. If you insist on living by the doctrines of yesterday, you are out of sync with reality. Every passing day you are drifting farther from the ability to control your world. I believe you have the right to live that way! But, do not condone (?) me by your definition of how I should live!

No addict goes into the use of drugs understanding its totality. They do not believe that drugs will take over their lives. People that accept alternative facts are no different. They use lies and untruths to escape from the pain of their everyday existence. They want to understand why they do not have jobs. They want greater acceptance. They do not understand why they cannot have what others have. There are a whole host of things they want for free. Accepting falsehoods creates a situation where there is no cost to easing their short run pain. In their minds, they are only seeking help to ease the hardship they live under. Logic, truth, and social convention describing the wisdom of abstaining from falsehoods are cast aside for a glimmer of hope. The problem is, it is false hope. People seek a painless costless way of supporting their way of life.

For the sake of argument, I will assume there is a linear relationship between accepting alternative facts and seeking a cheap form of help. It is like using drugs to ease the pain of reality. Obfuscating the truth and looking for easy answers only makes you less likely to control your environment. It does not solve problems. It creates problem. Let me present an example. I will use the pedagogy of arguing by exaggeration. I will make a simple generalization. Lies or untruths have infiltrated our social intercourse to such an extent that people live in an alternative reality. There are many political hot topics that politicians purport to be able to solve. However, to a religious person in Nebraska, or Ohio, or the South there is one major important directive in a person's life. It is their religion. It is the word of God. What is interesting is, most often, politically driven solutions are not the teachings of Catholicism. Solutions are not based on the teachings of Judaism. They are the teachings of Christian evangelism that are thrown about in the political arena. For the most part, evangelical life is directed by misogyny and an outdated set of values in their interpretation of the Bible. I will define misogyny as societal control by males. Man's purpose and that of God are in effect the letter of the Bible. But remember, society is dynamic. A literal interpretation of the Scripture is not applicable to reality.

Christian values are emotionally tied to the past. They are tied to a static world. Christians blindly follow alternative facts to validate their existence. The Christian right will follow whatever or whoever offers them religious stability as long as it is in their terms and, only their terms! Politicians like Donald Trump play to religious, political, and social discord. They offer cheap answers to people problems. Their words are hollow. They advocate a society where the voice of Christians is the only word that should be heard. Their interpretation of the Scriptures is that only the word of God is acceptable. Christians expect total freedom of expression at the expense of others. Here is an example. Remember, in the simplest of terms, taking a life is sinful. Christians view abortion as a form of execution or killing. They will not understand anyone else's position on the subject. They will not accept a woman's right to determine or define what should happen with her body. The Christian right is opposed to abortion. They are pro-life and support family values.

Children should be brought up in a two-parent household. They oppose Planned Parenthood. They deny the science of stem cell research and in vitro fertilization. They are opposed to contraception. In truth, Christians want to impose the male's to right to determine the sexual conduct of a woman. Christians want a stop to Roe v. Wade. They want to hear someone will strike down the 1973 Supreme Court ruling. They want to take away other people's rights and impose theirs. They deny other people's values! They consider them evil and want to make them illegal. They will not accept co-existing with other people's value judgments. They do not accept abortions as moral. You must follow their dictums or face God's retribution or the heavy hand of the law. Abortion must be illegal because their religion tells them so! Therefore, they want to impose their religious convictions on the state and make it illegal for everyone. Your faith or religious beliefs has no standing. They will not compromise! It is the word of God. This a good reason for the separation of church and state!

Let me present another example. Christian interpretation of the Bible is such that homosexual behavior is aberrant. They base their objections to homosexuality on the interpretation of the Bible. They use passages in the Bible such as Genesis 19.5, Romans 1: 26-27, Corinthians 6:9-10, 1 Timothy 1:10 and Jude 1:7 as a basis to establish a position on homosexuality. Homosexuality is so unacceptable that some religious groups try exerting their religious beliefs in foreign countries through proselytization. Uganda is an example. Christians advocate capital punishment for homosexual relations. Many Christians express the need for religious freedoms but are unalterably opposed to other people's religious freedoms.

Let us look at Donald Trump for a moment. He offers the Christian right a safe haven to thrust their religious values upon society. He offers them a platform to push their will upon society. Here is a Christian wish list:

1. Church and religious charities should be tax-exempt.
2. First Amendment rights to express political views in church.
3. Antiabortion pro-life stance.
4. Prayer in schools.
5. Opposition to gay rights.
6. The government will subsidize family values.

7. Denial of science.
8. The government making Christianity the United States' national religion.
9. Opposition to Planned Parenthood.
10. Opposition to stem cell research.
11. Bible studies in public schools.
12. No separation of church and state.
13. Opposition to sex education in public schools.
14. Support for the state of Israel.

Trump has issued presidential directives that allow churches to be involved in political advocacy and still remain tax-exempt. Vice President Pence is so misogynistic he will never allow a woman in his office without a male escort. He refuses to dine with women unless his wife is with him. His views on homosexuals are so archaic that he feels they can be educated to be heterosexual. He believes in the practices of curative intercourse and conversion therapy. His ideas are based on the Bible which is not dynamic instrument. He feels gays have a greater propensity for pedophilia. They are sexual predators. There is no proof of his convictions. He feels people can become homosexual because of environmental causes. There is no scientific proof of this hypothesis. He does not understand the science that shows 6% to 7% of all mammals are either homosexual or bisexual. Science accepts this mammalian behavior as normal not aberrant. However, Pence and Christians like him are still in the Dark Ages. They want to repress society. He is in lockstep with tenants or societal paradigms that are 2,000 years old. Pence views all decisions made relative women's rights should be deferred to Christian men. He is a faith-based believer.

Trump, on the other hand, has no religious beliefs. He is pragmatic at his core. He will say anything that will cultivate a political following. Both men espouse alternative facts or alternative truths as a way of gaining power. These two men, our President and Vice President, pander to the Christian right. They pander to people who are intolerant. They pander to people who have views that are stagnant in a dynamic world. What makes them and their Christian followers so dangerous is their self-righteousness and their inability to live in the real world. By accepting alternative facts, they are imposing their will upon others.

To show you how hypocritical the Christian right is they are willing to accept the indiscretions of a man like Donald Trump in order to gain their position of power in society. He does not live by their creed nor their faith. He is everything they do not stand for. But, Christians will sell their souls to be able to have the power to assert their will upon others. They will tie their allegiance to Trump no matter what he personally stands for and how he lives. All they care about is he gives them the hope of control. Remember what he stands for. He is a liar. He is an exploiter. He is misogynistic. He is a sexual predator. And, he is a person of no integrity.

Notwithstanding, the Christian right accepts him as a way of seeking control. There is a personal irony to the situation. My liberal beliefs tell me Christians have every right to espouse their religious beliefs. They have every right to feel the way they do. The problem is they do not have the right to dispel my rights and my freedoms. They asked me to be tolerant of their dispositions. They are not tolerant of mine. They are dismissive of the dynamic nature of time. Their belief system is predicated upon a stable state that was described 2,000 years ago in the Bible. They will try to force others to live by their standards and their interpretation of reality. What they embrace is stultifying. They live by archaic standards they are not in sync with reality. They expect us to do the same or face the punishment of their God. They are out of sorts with a dynamic world.

They do not accept science. They are fearful of technology. Christians are hateful of others. They are not compromising. They are crusaders willing to sacrifice life and limb for the past. As I have said before, I truly believe these people have the right of religious expression. I am happy for them to have something important to live by. I am hopeful, but not assured, they will respect my rights and my thoughts!

Donald Trump, a nonreligious person, is pandering to the need for certainty and stability of people who live in the past. Dynamism and change are viewed in the Christian community as the devil's work. Christians do not have the emotional stability to live in the real world. Therefore, they accept alternative facts and live in an alternative world. Donald Trump strikes an emotional chord with these provincial people. He tells them he will protect their way of life. It is ironic that he makes fools of them by living his life in the exact opposite of the teachings they profess. The Christian right and Donald J. Trump are made for each other! One is living a lie. The other tells lies.

Alternative Facts #18

Let us direct our attention to liberals. I will use a term to exemplify their progressive agenda. The term is welfare. Economists call welfare transfer payments. Welfare implies some type of greater good for society. It is generally the result of some kind of redistribution of income or wealth. Through government actions or programs there is the creation of greater opportunity and access for the masses. In reality, welfare is just a transfer payment. One person's earnings derived from the usage of land, labor, capital or entrepreneurial skills goes to another person. The intermediary is the government. The process is a subjective one. Who does society take from? Who does society give to? The decision is not always rational. It can be predicated upon social, political, ethnical, or racial biases. In any event, the giving class relinquishes their wealth involuntarily. The receiving class gets something for nothing. The progressive rationale for redistribution of wealth is simple. People with greater incomes should share their wealth with the disadvantaged. To tap a wealthy person's reservoir of wealth for the needy is the Hobbesian price of being a member of society. Transfer payments are a mechanism to even the playing field.

Conservatives who oppose welfare or transfer payments do not oppose the merits of helping others. They oppose the methodology. They feel the free market has a curative ability. Philanthropy and charity can bring about a more egalitarian society. Conservatives accept transfers on a personal not a governmental basis. They are not hard-hearted people. They feel their monies can be more efficiently directed to the needy if they are directed by the individual who earned the wealth.

Conservatives feel if someone competes in the marketplace and is successful, they should have the right to control their own wealth. They can, and will, donate money or goods and services in kind if they so desire. It is a voluntary exercise. It should not be mandatory through a tax imposition. Charity and philanthropy should not be in the province of government. Conservatives feel the notion of welfare is subjective. It is predicated upon individual altruism. Liberals or progressives want to make redistribution of income a function of government. It is an involuntary societal duty to help the disadvantaged. The rich must give to the poor. It is the cost of being successful! In both cases, there is an acceptance of transference of wealth. But, as discussed earlier, the two competing political philosophies are at odds. Should transfers be free market driven or government directed? Americans as a whole feel charity is part of our Judea-Christian heritage. The question is how the monies are collected and who should they be distributed to.

Now, let us look at the liberal model. Liberals or progressives feel people are unsuccessful because of a lack of opportunity. They predicate their ideas upon the concept of imperfect competition. Progressives take the position that sellers take advantage of buyers. Owners take advantage of workers. The rich take advantage of the poor. The only way the playing field can even out is through government intervention. The government should tax the sellers, the owners, and the rich. Monies, or services, should be transferred to the losers in the imperfect marketplace. The beneficiaries of welfare or transfer payment should be the worker, the consumer, and the poor. Liberals feel a tax upon the rich should be progressive. It will only marginally hurt the rich because they have enough wealth or income to offset the transfer of money. This is a subject value judgment. People that are taxed are rich. They can afford it. The little pain the wealthy class feels is small compared to the benefits the poor, the consumer, and the worker receive.

Here is an example. Liberals in California have passed legislation called a Millionaire's Tax. If someone has an annual income of $1 million a year, or $83,500 a month or more, they should pay 1% more in state income taxes. This tax generates over $200 million a year. Let me give you an example. Monies are specifically directed to subsidizing housing for the poor, section #8. The idea is simple. Every Californian deserves a place to live. It is a societal guarantee. It is a right not a privilege. Taking what amounts to a pittance from the rich and giving to the poor will solve the housing problem. It is evident the market place cannot feed and house all members of society. It never has. Take a little from the rich. They can afford it! This sounds reasonable. This sounds good to the progressive minded. The problem is, in many cases the poor take advantage of what is given to them. Welfare can be a disincentive. Why work for food and shelter if it is free? Why help people who refuse to help themselves? Why help out the losers? In subsidizing rents, there is no incentive to take care of the properties. Why take care of something if you have no responsibilities of ownership? Why work for $10 dollars an hour if you can receive $10 dollars or more in government aid with little or no strings attached.

Liberals do not understand the concept of self-reliance and hard work. They do not understand the concept of "if I can do it why can't they?" They refuse to make people responsible for their own actions or inactions. They do not allow for people losing in a competitive world. In their minds, everyone must be a winner. Everyone gets a trophy! The world is not egalitarian. In reality, not everyone deserves help - especially when it comes at someone else's expense

Let me get back to the idea of alternative truths and how they reinforce philosophies. Liberals live in a world of alternative facts when it comes to wealth. They feel that your wealth is theirs. They feel income and wealth are dirtied by the way people win in the market place. They resent rich people. In the above example of housing, liberals will discuss the benefits of government subsidies. They never discuss the blight, the gangs, and social decay caused by government housing. They will never discuss how welfare diminishes a person's competitive position in the marketplace. Again, why work for $10 or $15 an hour when you can get a welfare check and not have to work at all? You have heard on many occasions that welfare payments are no more than a form of plantation economics. People on welfare never get off of it. They are subjected to a second-class existence. Their offspring become future generations of welfare recipients as well. Welfare does not create opportunities for people to get skills. It does not change the climate and culture of poverty. There is an adage: it is better to teach a person how to fish then give them food. Welfare does not better person's life. It is no more than a bandage.

Liberals feel the majority of welfare recipients are worthy of help because of their circumstances. They earn less than the poverty line. Because of a lack of opportunity, they do not have the skills to compete in the marketplace. Therefore, they do not make enough income to purchase the necessities of life. It is not their fault because of institutional barriers or obstacles and they have not been given a chance. Hence, the need for the government to subsidize them. But, and there always a but - out of hand liberals dismiss the realities of laziness, fraud, anti-social behavior, and a whole host of reasons for people not putting in an effort but receiving government assistance. Statistically anywhere from 12% to 14% of welfare recipients are taking advantage of welfare program. We will call this welfare fraud.

Estimates of 10% levels of welfare fraud come from *The Economist* magazine, May 31, 2014, to as high as 20% welfare fraud from *Politifact*, January 20, 2014. Most professional economists are comfortable with a 12% to 14% range. We will euphemistically call people who commit fraud *freeloaders*. These people are unworthy of our help. Liberals distance themselves from this fact. They minimize fraud. They minimize the fact that welfare creates a class of unproductive people.

Let us look at reality. For the most part 85% to 90% of welfare recipients are worthy. More than 25% of recipients are under the age of 12. They cannot work. More than 40% are above the age of 65 and they cannot work. Approximately 35% to 40% of welfare recipients are in the age groups that allows them to be employable. Many, but not all of them, seek employment. Let me politicize those figures. The actual statistics on welfare recipients looks like this: they are young; they are old; most recipients are not of working age. And, the vast majority, 65% to 70%, are white and rural. I want you to reflect on how you have been brainwashed in your understanding of who they are. Remember alternative truths. For political reasons, people who receive welfare are considered to be unworthy. They do not deserve it. People should not have to pay for them out of their hard-earned money. No one likes to be taxed to pay for someone who is taking advantage of us. Using your mind's eye, paint a visual picture of people on welfare. It will not be factual but it will be comforting as it will give you someone to hate. Someone who is lesser than you! Remember exclusion. You will inevitably picture a minority person. If he is black, he will be menacing looking. He will be of working age and, he will be taking your money for doing nothing and will never appreciate it. If she is a black woman, she will be using her welfare check or food stamps to buy goods you do not approve of. The more babies she has, the more money she gets. She will be loud and uneducated.

If your picture is that of a Hispanic, she will be Mexican. She will be illegal. She is young and pregnant. She already has 4 to 5 children and not taking care of them the way you would. If your picture is of someone who is white, you will be in the minority. Your white person is receiving unemployment insurance. He or she can work. But, and again there is always a but - they do not want to work. If your picture is that of a crackhead or someone who takes methamphetamines, they are someone who is too high to work. Your picture of all these welfare recipients is way off line. It does not comport with reality. Very few people you picture to be on the welfare roll actually exist. Maybe 10 to 12%, but your alternative truths say otherwise. You willing to believe the lies so you do not have to sacrifice for another person. But, for the grace of God, you could be on the welfare roll. However, since you are not, why should you care? Why should give up your money to some ingrate?

Let us look at a mixed economy. Understand it cannot produce enough jobs to fill employment needs. If we look at the statistics, there is anywhere from 10% to 15% structural employment for low skilled workers. Liberals distance themselves from the fact some of these people are so low skilled they are not employable. They will not even discuss the basic question of who is at fault - is it that a person has low skill levels? The market determines that wages have to be lower than a wage earner's rates of production. No one will rationally pay a worker more than what they are worth. If employers have to do this, it causes unemployment, lower profits or inflation. Historically, this occurs when employment is above 96%. This is called the *normative rate of unemployment*. Liberals also rationalize away any selfish nature of people wanting to take advantage of welfare. They turn their eyes away from people who are too lazy to work and from people who want to game the system. They do not take into consideration that some people expect something for nothing. Another problem is liberals do not understand that some recipients do not appreciate the sacrifices other people make. They do not understand why people resent giving their wealth to others who they feel are unworthy of help.

There is another alternative reality for liberals. They do not understand that welfare can create a situation where people are actually worse off. Because of government aid, some people won't learn the skills to be self-sufficient. Many welfare recipients never learn how to fend for themselves. It is easier for them to accept mere tokens than work hard. They do not correlate work with the ability to have a better life. Liberals do not understand that welfare can take people's incentive away. Many welfare recipients become the prisoners of society. They never advance. They are imprisoned or enculturated into a second-class status. In their eyes, there is no chance or reason for personal advancement. They have never seen it. They pass their anger and bitterness on to their offspring. Welfare most often creates a culture of dependency. Liberals deny this fact. I must reiterate that a small percentage of welfare recipients, 10% to 12%, take advantage of it. But, and there is always a but – political welfare fraud and lazy people are a picture we see in the welfare state. Sadly, it is a small percentage of bad apples that define the bushel.

In reality, the percentage of fraudulent welfare recipients is small in number. The problem is their reflection on the political landscape is overstated. Conservatives exaggerate welfare fraud. On the other side, liberals live in a false reality. They do not accept the failure of transfer payments. They are no different than the religious right when it comes to clarity.

Alternative Facts #19

Alternative facts are an authoritarian way to attempt to control society. Lies and falsehoods are little more than hyperbole of ideological based people to get their way. The resulting fear created by the dissemination of alternative facts can be immense. Make up eminent threats and spread them the right way and people will follow. Right wing conservatives are ideological. It is easier for them to make up facts. The ends legitimize the means. Left wing radicals are more principled based. They do not lie as much and when they do, it is more situational. Both groups have elevated their deluge of lies to historical heights. Professional opinion makers on both sides have been successful in pushing political agendas. Spin masters have the ability to get the public to believe the political elites can protect citizens from uncertainties and instability. Politicians create a world the shelters people from their greatest fears. Socio biologists have known for years that humans are afraid of randomness. Our response to the danger of the unknown is finding patterns that alleviate our fears. Alternative facts are comforting. They dispel our deep-seated fears. It is ironic that in today's political environment, people's fears are created by the very people who lie about curing societal ills. Today, conservatives talk about the ills of globalization. In truth, they had been advocates of this policy for years. Conservatives praise the trickle-down theory as a way of bringing up the standard of living of the middle class. Again, this is ironic. There is no truth that trickle-down or supply-side economics ameliorate a poor distribution of wealth.

As a case in point, let us look at the trickle-down theory. I have previously discussed the theoretical construct of this 1930's theory: Say's law, the Pigou effect, automatic restoration to equilibrium, and the classical model of pure competition. They are the bases for the trickle-down theory. In summation, supply creates demand. This is supply-side economics. It became popular again after the Great Depression with Arthur Laffer and the Ronald Reagan administration in the 1980's. The Great Depression and its after effects proved the trickle-down theory did not work. In the simplest of terms, supply-side economics states, if the entrepreneurial class receive benefits, these benefits will trickle down to the people below them. Economic growth needs more labor, usage of land, and more capital. The government can facilitate economic growth by giving money to the rich. They will invest their newfound money. When entrepreneurs put their money in these factors of production, the economy will expand. This increase in supply will create greater remunerations for the factors of production. A bigger base of wages, rents, and interest rate payments will result from stimulating investment. As the entrepreneurial class expands the economy, wealth trickles down to the other factors of production. Primarily, the wage earner. This sounds good! However, there is little or no evidence that it actually happens in relative terms.

There is no historical evidence that the trickle-down theory is an economic reality. It is no more than an alternative truth. It is no more than a lie. It is a way of creating a pattern for people who want to believe there is equal opportunity and possible advancement within economic growth. The positive pattern of the trickle-down theory is wages go up. This is the positive re-enforcement for the wage earner. In reality, inflation will eat up all income gains but this pattern is hard to see. Also, the pattern of relative gains is not as noticeable. The rich get richer at a faster pace than wage earners earning.

In reality, supply-side economics should be called the *urination theory*. By giving the rich more access to money, the economy will flourish. Lower interest rates, lower taxes, and greater government subsidies will expand the economy. But, and there is always a but - this type of economic expansion through government intervention redistributes the wealth. The rich become better off in relative and absolute terms compared to the middle or poor classes. The rich gain more when the economy goes up and loses less when the economy goes down. In absolute and relative terms, the trickle-down theory is no more than a way of giving more wealth to the rich. Higher profits coupled with inflationary prices create a greater distance between the rich and the middle and the poor. Instead of calling it the trickle- down some people say the rich are pissing down on the middle and the poor.

With the amount of accepted statistical evidence and published literature, it is incomprehensible that people still buy into the trickle-down theory. People are grasping for a pattern or a cure that will promise them a better future. They are looking for a pattern. In truth, they are willing to buy into any lie that portends a better future. People think higher wages $20 an hour instead of $10 wakes them better off. That is not generally the case with inflation. Workers are usually worse off or better off at a lesser rate than the rich.

People that are not intellectually curious are seeking simple solutions. They think higher wage make them better off. That is not the case. Inflation is insidious. Many people are not educationally engaged enough to realize truth from lies. They actually believe the trickle-down theory will help the worker. Some people are so lacking in reliable sources of knowledge they are not reality bound. It is harsh, but we must blame them for their decision-making. Under our breath, we view them as idiots, morons, or cretins. But, and there is always a but - they view us in a similar way. They look at our sources of information as flawed. They are right! We are wrong in our views of the trickle-down theory. They think we are ingesting falsehoods no matter how science based the facts are. There is a name for it.

Conservatives call our progressive sources of information "fake news." Our information, for the most part, comes from the traditional media. Outlets like *CNN*, *National Public Radio*, *New York Times*, and *The Washington Post*. Until recently, they were historically viewed as objective. No longer! The right view them as fake news or alternative truths. The progressive may have a more scholarly way of appraising things but to the other side it is no more than lies. Conservatives and progressives both think they are right. They both think the other side buys into an unacceptable alternative reality.

Two different interpretations and two different
realities of the same facts. I will say most
Americans are not equipped to understand
the truth. If that is the case, we have a
problem! We cannot and must not tamper
with people's inalienable rights to express
their views no matter how foolish we they
think they are. We must rethink how we
generate and distribute information if we are
to keep our freedoms. We must stop the lies
and deceit that permeate the very bedrock of
our society. We face a perplexing problem.
How do we deal with the threat of our loss
of freedom when people are dumb as dirt
and buy into lies? How do we govern and for
what purpose?

Alternative Facts #20

Global warming is real. There is no scientific evidence to refute its existence. There are no short run solutions to alter the damage it will do to humankind. There is no science to alter the eminent danger posed by climate change. We have nothing in our arsenal of scientific weapons to stop the impending catastrophes posed by the heating up of the Earth. All we can do is try to slow it down. We have passed the tipping point. The question that remains is why do people oppose the science? Why do they not accept the inevitability of global warming?

Why did President Trump pull the United States out of the Paris Climate Accord? Why are we one of three nations who are not in alignment with the rest of the world concerning the protection of future generations? The other two are Syria and Nicaragua. The accord will limit the use of carbon-based fuels. It will push the consumption of carbon-based fuels back to 1992 levels. The accord's ultimate goal will be to limit the increase in temperature to 2° Fahrenheit over the next 100 years. Putting this in layman's terms, the average global temperature is approximately 59°. If the accord is not implemented, the world temperature will increase to 61° to 63°. It is imperative that hydrocarbon emissions are limited to save the Earth as we know it. Higher temperatures will cause the following major problems:

Climate change: Causing droughts, flooding, wild fires, food shortages, and the melting of the ice caps.

Changes in the Earth biodiversity: Extinction of many species, both fauna and flora.

Ocean acidification: Destruction of the coral reefs and lowering of the fish production for food and fertilizer. Acid rain: Polluting soil and land. Health issues: Migration of insects, animals and bacteria causing epidemics.

The problems cut across all human boundaries. They affect all nations and their peoples. They affect both genders. Income has no relevance - climate change affects both the rich and the poor. The problems caused by global warming are universal. Science is clear and unwavering.

Global warming is real and must be attended to. But, and there is always a but - some Americans, led by Donald Trump, deny the science. They do not accept the eminent dangers posed by man-made hydrocarbons polluting the atmosphere. They lie to protect their position of standing in society. They lie to keep the status quo. Many of the lies are based on religious interpretation of the Bible. Many of the lies are predicated upon profit maximization where the short run takes precedence over the long run. Falsehoods are disseminated to create powerful political positions. Approximately 36% to 42% of the electorate have bought into these lies. For the most part, anti-climate change deniers are conservatives. In particular, they are the alt right and evangelical Christians. These groups are unanimous in their desire to pull the United States out of the Paris Accord. I will present some of their flawed reasoning. Please make note of the fact that their analysis is predicated upon lies. Their rational is not based on facts. Their views are dangerous not only to the present generation but to future generations.

As we have discussed earlier, alternative truths are used to protect a person's value system or his or her way of life. Emulation, a hurried leisurely life, and a person's genetic makeup are major contributors to how a person views reality. Ideology and principles also play a major role in creating clarity. All of the above are the driving forces of alternative truths. In the case of global warming, lies have also been monetized. There are whole industries generating lies to make money. This is evidenced by organizations like Breitbart. Many of their ideas are infused into Christian dogma. Their ideas are even in the platforms of the Republican Party. Republicans deny global warming. Democrats, on the other hand, embrace the science and ask for more government control over the use of carbon-based fuels. These two parties are diametrically and diabolically opposed in the visions of how science relates to global warming. On the conservative side, there are denials and the out of hand dismissal of science. Conservatives have created unwarranted doubts of science's veracity. The Republican propaganda machine has effectively persuaded 36% to 40% of the electorate that global warming does not exist. The Democrats quite often overstate its effects but accept the science.

The deniers of climate change are willing to let untold numbers of future generations die. This is not hyperbole. This is fact. The only thing in question is how many people will die and under what circumstances. The same people also believe that global warming will create a loss of economic activity and jobs. This, too, is refutable. A case in point is the coal miners. Arguments are made that what goes for coal goes for the whole energy sector. There might be a loss of some jobs. It will be minimal when taking into consideration the emergence of renewable sources of energy. It could be minimal if federal dollars go into retraining and welfare payments. In any event, unemployment caused by attacking the causes of global warming will be small. But, and there always is a but - how many jobs? Where are they located? What are the politics in the states where there is impending unemployment? Can workers be retrained and at what cost? Here are some numbers to reflect on. The Bureau of Labor estimates that entire US energy sector only employer 2.8 million workers. At present, total American employment is estimated to be 162,000,000 workers.

Energy accounts for approximately 2% 0f all employment in the United States. In the traditional production of oil, coal, and natural gas there are 1,100,000 workers. There are 980,000 workers in the distribution of fossil fuels. These are gas station workers. These are also people who facilitate the distribution of electricity and natural gas. We also have workers who deal in the retail end of energy. Finally, there are 800,000 workers in the low emission energy field, renewables. Solar is the largest followed by nuclear. In the energy sector, coal is the most politically relevant. However, we are only talking about 350,000 workers. If one coal miner loses his or her job, it is too many in personal terms. We must understand that. But, to save jobs today, that kills off our future we must understand that is an unacceptable as well. We can retrain worker who lose their jobs. There is a present-day cost but future saving in human terms. There are also age restrictions placed upon employment. If unemployed workers are too old, we must give them transfer payments. We will just call the payments "Extended and Enhanced Social Security payments." If the unemployed workers are not mobile, we must bring industry to them. These are small costs relative to destroying our environment by continuing to use fossil fuels. If coal miners lose their jobs, their transfer payment costs are short run and diminish over time. In the long run, they are small compared to the damage done to the environment.

There are many reasons people believe combating global warming is foolish. Some climate change deniers believe that accepting the science behind global warming is in direct conflict with biblical teachings. Some believe that destroying Barack Obama's legacy is important enough to accept the denial of science. Maybe the most important reason for doubting science is if you accept the lies you do not have to do anything but stay the course. There is an old adage, "if there is no solution there is no problem!" For many science deniers, they are willing to accept the consequences of lies because the costs are in the distant future. It is easier than changing their lives and making sacrifices today.

Deniers know deep down inside what the truth is. But, and there is always a but - deniers are too selfish to sacrifice for others. They refuse to accept science because it will change their lives. Change is threatening. It creates instability and uncertainty. The status quo, staying the same, is more acceptable. People accept alternative truths because it is easier and less threatening than solving the problem.

The science is clear. It is only the timing and the level of destruction that are debatable. The impact of global warming and the catastrophes that will follow are only debatable in relative terms. There is absolute scientific proof that global warming will be disastrous. Some deniers equate the progressive messages of the left to crying Wolf. They will not accept the narrative of change because they are opposed to outside forces telling them what to do. Here is a brief list of reasons why people oppose the concept of global warming. Most of these alternative truths are pushed out upon the public by the fossil fuel industry. We also have the Koch brothers, Jim Inofe, the Center for Media and Democracy, the State Policy Network, and Rupert Murdoch's Fox media conglomerate. There are many other disseminators of alternative facts. Most are on the right. The left believes in science. Deniers of science contradict the inevitability of the problems caused by climate change. Here is a list of some of the reasons why people challenge the science behind climate change.

1. No significant long run climate data exists. Only short run data - less than 150 years.
2. Deniers doubt human activities are large enough to cause temperature changes. The vast

majority of hydrocarbons, 95%, are created by natural causes.

3. CO2 has no measurable impact on climate change.
4. There is no data that global warming is harmful. We are in a cycle Global warming is cyclical.
5. Global warming is a national problem not a world problem. There are no polycentric solutions to national problems. The free marketplace will solve global warming.
6. People who care about the environment are left-wing socialists.
7. Dealing with climate change will infringe upon civil liberties.
8. Solutions to climate change are job killing activities.
9. The problem is that climate change over estimated. Scare mongering.
10. Climate change is an atheist ploy to grab power.

Alternative Facts #21

People who buy into alternative facts are denying the existence of truths, evidence, and science. Previously we discussed climate change. Conservatives disregarded science and led by Donald Trump America removed itself from the Paris Accord. The welfare of future generations was not a consideration for the ideologues of the right.

Jobs and profits won over the environment and the welfare of our children. Keeping this in mind, now I want to talk about another undeniable truth. I want to talk about President Trump's wall. The wall that many Americans, 36% to 40%, think will solve the problems of illegal immigration. Instead of denying science, people who believe in the efficacy of the wall deny evidence. They are denying the truth as it applies to illegal immigration.

Let me start by saying there are estimates of upwards of 20,000,000 people who domicile in America illegally. They came upon our shores by a night and have remained here as illegal residents. That is not refutable! That is a fact! There is empirical evidence to back up the illegal mass migration of people on to our shores. We have statistics that in the 1990's over 3,000 people a day were illegally crossing from Mexico into California. This is a fact. Let me paint a picture that is usually not part of the narrative of illegal immigration. The border between the United States and Mexico is continuous and unbroken for almost 2,100 miles. What is remarkable and almost never stated publicly is the fact that this border has the greatest differential of incomes of any border in the world. The average Mexican has a per capita income of $3,156 as measured by the USDA Foreign Agricultural Service in 2016. The average American has a per capita income of almost $52,000 as measured by the Department of Labor. Per capital income is GDP divided by population. We are looking at $18.5 trillion divided by 320,000,000 people.

The second largest disparity of incomes between neighboring nations is Bangladesh and India. Incomes are $478 for Bengalis and $1,610 for Indians as measured, again, by the Department of Labor. I want you to make a personal reflection of what you think of India - how wealthy are they compared to us? Now, reflect on Bangladesh. How many Bengalis cross into India - an India stop them with a wall?

The differential between the United States and Mexico is quantum. Most borders that house opposing nations look like United States versus Canada. Note, our per capita incomes are almost similar. Canada's per capita income is almost $46,000 versus that of the United States at $52,000. We are not only similar in wealth, we are similar and culture and traditions. This is the general rule for neighboring countries. Proximity equates to similarity. Vancouver and Seattle could be sister cities. That is not the case between San Diego and Tijuana. Mexicans want to come here. We are rich. They are poor. Canadians are like us. Both peoples are similar.

Let me now shift from descriptive to theoretical. The second law of thermodynamics is a concept called *entropy*. Objects in a higher pressure isolated system seek lower pressured systems. This can be observed by thinking about the air pressure in the tire of your car. A nail enters into the wall of you tire. Air from the high-pressure tire, 35 to 40 pounds per square inch, flow out to the ambient environment which is of lesser pressure per square inch. You can hear the sound of the air moving from high to low. This is the entropy at work. This is true of people as well. People that live in Mexico live in a highly dense poverty-stricken environment. They want to live in areas where the pressure is less. More wealth and greater opportunity exist in the United States. This is called social entropy. The question is how do we fight the social science of people wanting to get to a better place in life?

I will present an example of the difference in living conditions between Tijuana, Mexico and Southern California. For people who live in San Diego, Carlsbad, Solana Beach, or any of the neighboring cities in San Diego County, all have one thing in common - they are absolutely and relatively wealthier than their counterparts in Mexico who live only a few miles away. As a Southern Californian, you decide to go on a day trip to Tijuana. It is simple. Take a half an hour or 45-minute drive south. You are at the border ready to go into one of Mexico's largest cities. The first thing you have to consider is where will you park your car? Is it the U.S. side of the border or the Mexican side of the border? What are the insurance implications of both driving and parking in Mexico? For most Americans, they take the easier choice of leaving their car on the American side. The next thing to take into consideration is walking across the border to get into Mexico. The border is more than a line. It is a neutral zone with wire fences on both sides. It is approximately 200 feet from one country to the other. Besides fences, there are border guards to check for identification. There are also sophisticated electronics. All you do is walk through the checkpoint on the United States side of the border to a checkpoint on the Mexican side. In less than 1 or 2 minutes, you are in Mexico.

Once you cross the border, you are in a new world. Even though Mexico is statistically an immediately developed nation, you sense the abject poverty. There are children begging for money. You have seen street people before, but these beggars are different. They are a different definition of poor. The streets are unkempt. The smells are different. The sounds are different. You are in a poor, threatening environment. Let me reflect back to the border crossing for one second. As you are crossing the 200-foot check point, you realize you have to use a bathroom. You are between two countries. Do you venture forward to Mexico? Or, will you back track to the United States? You relieve yourself and again find that you are hungry? Do you venture forward to buy food from a kiosk on the street in Mexico? Or, you go back and buy taco at Taco Bell on the American side? Again, you find yourself between the two countries and you are thirsty. Do you venture forward and buy a bottle of water under a Mexican brand name? Or, would you back track and go to the United States and look for a drinking fountain or buy a bottle of Arrowhead water? Let me put all this together. Whose social facilities do you use? Whose food do you eat? Whose water do you drink? It is clear. It is evident. There is a huge disparity between the United States and Mexico. They are only 200 feet from us but you know their food, water and social facilities are inferior! Also, you realize that Mexico is not only poor, it has one of the worst distributions of wealth in the world.

There are clear distinctions between Mexicans. Mexicans with European blood, either Spanish or French, are generally wealthier than indigenous peoples of American Indian descent. Mexico has one of the highest crime rates in the world. Chances of advancement for the average Mexican in social and economic terms are minimal. Whatever you are born into is where you stay. Mexican mortality and morbidity rates are higher than that in America. Educational rates are grossly different. Less than 5% of all Mexicans attend university. Whereas, in the United States, more than 60% of adults have university or technical training. There are many other differences that make Mexicans want to come to America. We will just say that Mexico is a country distinctively different than the United States. One last piece of information - Mexico's rate of unemployment is more than 60%.

Take all of this in the consideration and where would you rather be? There is another question. Whose fault is it that Mexico is poor? Who is their biggest trading partner? Who waged war against them in 1848? Who annexed large swaths of their land? A more contemporary question - do you really think that USMCA, the new North American Trade Agreement, is really disadvantageous to the United States and the deal is better for Mexico? We will discuss the tenants of these questions in greater detail later. Let me get back to the case in point. The difference between the United States and Mexico is easily evidenced by a cursory visual examination. Mexico's conditions are so bad that millions of their people are willing to sacrifice life and limb to get to a place of greater security and opportunity. Mexicans would literally die to get to the United States. They would die to give their children a greater opportunity in life. But, for the grace of God, it could be you. You could have been born in Mexico. What would you do to protect your children if you were born in Tijuana? Could a wall stop you? Can anything stop social entropy? The border between Mexico and the US reflects no more than a high pressure versus a low pressure area. A little pinhole that euphemistically popped the tire can create a situation where millions of people flow into the United States. That pinhole is the opportunity of economic and social advancement.

Alternative Facts #21A

Let me add some real facts to our discussion of the wall. There is little, or no, economic loss because of illegal immigration as presented by the Office of Policy Planning in the US Immigration and Naturalization Service. They estimate a wash at the low end and a $10.3 billion taxpayers' expense at the high end. The net cost of illegal immigration is offset by the taxes and increase economic activity generated by the illegal workers. You hear arguments about welfare, policing costs, educational costs, and health and welfare costs. These costs are real and calculable. For the most part, they are not exaggerated. But, and there is always a but - these costs are offset by taxes collected from illegal workers primarily on their consumption.\

There are 22 major local, state, and federal taxes. The largest generators of revenue for government are income tax, corporate and business taxes, and sales taxes. Other major taxes include payroll taxes, user's taxes, tariffs, customs, duties, lottery taxes, OMV, liquor, cigarette, gasoline taxes, and assorted levies on either income or consumption. In aggregate taxes arc regressive in nature. People at the lowest quartile of income pay a higher percentage of their earnings than the top quartile of income earners. Most illegal immigrants are not paying income nor payroll taxes. They are not paying Social Security taxes. They are, however, paying sales taxes and a host of other indirect taxes. Most of their taxes are on consumption.

Let me present an example. As usual, I

will argue by exaggeration. Many manual laborers are illegal. They take low-paying jobs American citizens would not consider endeavoring in. We will look at an illegal worker who waits in front of Home Depot for someone to secure his services. He may haul garbage or refuse. He may do landscaping. He or she may do domestic work at your home. In any of the above cases, you pay them in cash. Neither he nor you pay Social Security. No taxes are collected for unemployment insurance. In essence, their income is tax-free. But, he does in fact pay taxes. He pays a good deal of his income in hidden taxes. Everything, except the food he consumes, has a sales tax or a value added tax imposed upon it. Keep in mind indirect taxes that are levied upon sellers of products but paid by the consumer. We refer to whoever pays the tax as the incidence of tax. We look at the taxpayer not who the tax is levied upon. An example of this is as a renter in most market situations, you pay the property taxes levied upon the owner's dwellings. Any time government increases the tax on gasoline to the producers, they pass it on to the consumer. If you pool all the tax dollars that the poor or, in this case illegal aliens pay, they are regress. These tax dollars offset the cost of illegal immigration. Illegals in this country pay for the education costs, health and welfare costs, law enforcement costs, and any cost the host nation has to pay for their illegal domicile. The revenue generated through taxation roughly equates to the cost associated with illegal immigration. It is a wash!

People who enter into the United States illegally historically are the best of the disadvantaged from their home country. They face criminal penalties in both their home countries and the countries they are illegally migrating to. They face the prospects of injury or death in the journey to a better place. In Darwinian terms, they are the fittest of their kind. Not only physically but mentally. When they arrive in America, the culture they bring to our shores is the fabric that has made us great. I will use Mexicans as an example. They are religious people. They are family oriented. Their families are intact. The last component of their desirable characteristics is that they are hard workers. The only thing they have lacked is opportunity in their home countries. Statistically, first-generation immigrants are law abiding citizens. They are more lawful than the average American. They are religious. In the example of Mexicans, they are Catholic. They are hardworking. They are not drags upon society as portrayed by the conservative right.

A point of enlightenment. There is a saying that it is better to pay now than pay later. I will use this concept in relationship to illegal immigration. The social law of entropy tells us that people will cross the borders to seek a better life. We cannot stop them. There are no borders that will hold between states of unequal pressure. Entropy is irrefutable. It is immutable. Thus, we should make illegal migrants an asset when they arrived here and not a liability. We cannot stop the laws of science so we should take advantage of them. Most demographic studies show that the United States population is getting older. Our birth rates are declining. This is a function of income as well as the changing of our cultural norms. We will face a shortage of labor in the future and our needs for employable people must come from somewhere. We cannot expect technology in the forms of automation and cybernetics to mollify our need for more workers. We must monitor immigration and it has to be orderly. Prospective workers, through education, must be made more productive. Thus, we can make illegals and asset. We should give them assistance in shelter, food, education, and health as a basis for citizenship. They must be enculturated into the American lifestyle.

If we give them the opportunity of education, they will indeed become assets. They will be the future generation of American workers that make our country great again. We should expect them to follow our cultural norms and abide by our laws. There should be a process by which they become legal - they should not be allowed to come here and be a liability which could be the case if they cross our borders illegally. We cannot allow them to become second-class citizens. They must work for citizenship. If we pay for them now, they will be productive Americans. We will not have to pay for their transgression later as illegal aliens or second-class citizen. With opportunity, they will become lawful citizens and the backbone of our economy.

The reality of today is illegals sneak across our border. They seek jobs no one else will take. They will accept lower wages because they are not educated and are lacking in skills. Many, over time, will not flourish in our economy. If they are not given assistance, they will become second-class citizens and will be relegated to poverty and crime. If we do not bring them into our society in an orderly way, they will become a liability. We will incur huge welfare costs. We will incur huge policing costs. Society will be bifurcated between legals that are wealthy and illegals that are poor. If we do not spend money and bring illegals into our society, they will remain poor. They will not assimilate and reach the potential as legal citizens. If they are not afforded opportunities, they remain poor. Poorer people have higher birth rates, commit more crimes, and have greater health problems.

They will also be become liabilities and the problem of illegal immigration will exacerbate over time. We must pay up front and bring them in in an orderly fashion. We must give them a path to citizenship. If we do, our cost will be lower than creating a nation of illegal immigrants. If we make them a liability, they will be a cost burden for future generations.

I would hope you understand immigrants can be assets. Very few are drug traffickers and gang members. Estimates are less than 1.5% of all illegals that cross our borders are murderers, rapists, and gangsters as portrayed by the conservative right - a political mistruth. As I have said earlier, the people who want to come to our shores are the best. They only want what we have. They have asked for opportunities and the ability to gain entrance into our culture. It is foolhardy not to embrace them and their future contributions. The wall that Donald Trump wants to build will not stop them from coming into this country. In the long run, no wall has ever been successful in stopping migration. Certainly, the biggest wall of them all, The Great Wall of China, did not work. The law of entropy tells us there are no long run barriers to entry. A wall will not stop people. Parenthetically, the wall is more than just a physical structure. It is a way of creating a second-class citizen. It is the height of asininity to think that Donald Trump will get Mexico to pay for the wall. There are no historical precedents. If they do, in fact, pay for the wall, the economic consequences will diminish the Mexican economy. Hence, more illegal immigration. More Mexicans will want to come into the United States if Mexico's economy sputters. In all likelihood, the wall will be more than a physical structure. A major component of the wall will be the electronics for surveillance of people coming across into the United States. It will not be 2,100 miles in length. The geography is such that there are stretches of badlands that are impassable. The picture of a wall like the Great Wall of China is a misrepresentation.

There is another component to why this wall is not reasonable. Worldwide, the cost of traveling from point A to point B has dropped dramatically. That is not only for the rich but also for all components of society. We have technology that promotes travel and communication at very low costs. It is difficult to understand a situation where people cannot go from one place to another when technology makes travel so accessible to the average person. They only real barriers are political.

Many illegals can gather enough money to travel to America for business or tourism.

Obviously, these are not the abject poor. They are middle-class or wealthy foreign nationals. They travel to our shores and extend their stays to permanency. For many, it is cheap to fly over or sail around the wall. In reality, the wall is just a complex of electronics and algorithms that monitor the coming and goings of people. The intrinsic cost of enforcing who is here and how long they stay is prohibitive - it is not who illegally comes to America that poses the problem. The problem is how to make them assets. If we ignore them, they become liabilities. There is no evidence that illegals are more prone to breaking the laws and engaging in criminal activities that actual American citizens. There is no statistical evidence that they are liabilities. If they become liabilities, it is of our making.

When illegals come to our shores the vast majority are poor and uneducated. As we have said earlier, they are seeking opportunities and a better place for themselves and their families. Initially they take the lowest paying jobs. There is a black market for illegal workers. But, and there is always a but - they take jobs that Americans do not want or will not take. It is not only because of the poor rates of remuneration but also because of the undesirability of the work. Immigration, legal or illegal, is a good thing because it allows for people to fill niche jobs that Americans will not partake in.

There are many reasons why we try to keep illegal immigrants from entering our country. Obviously, there is bigotry towards people who are not like us. There are people who are not willing to pay now and embrace the wave of social entropy. There are many political considerations. These and many other factors are the bases of alternative truths about the nature of illegal immigrants. We should be proud of them and embrace them. We should allow them to have the same opportunities that we are granted through our citizenship. Citizenship for all good standing people that live in America should be a right. It should not only be a privilege for the people who were born here.

There is one last component to this complex problem of illegal immigration. Even if the political tide is strong enough to build the wall and not allow people in, it is wrong! Even if the political tides are strong enough to deport people that have illegally domiciled on our shores, it is wrong! The laws of entropy tell us so. But, and there is always a but - politics tells us Mexicans are a burden and we must rid ourselves of them. Politics tells us we must extricate them from society. The question is how do we keep them out and deport them back to Mexico? What is the cost of deporting millions of people? What resources are at our disposal to effectuate actual deportation? Is it fiscally viable? Who takes the jobs of the displaced immigrants who are no longer part of our job market? Realize that walling off a country and deporting illegals is contrary to the second law of thermodynamics. In the short run, under the current administration, we have seen actual rates of people trying to illegally come to our country drop. This is a fact. I maintain that this is a short run anomaly. In the long run, the laws of social entropy will take over. In the long run, nothing can stop people from seeking a better life and, in the long run, there must be opportunities to allow for a better distribution of wealth for all. Alternative facts can only hide the real problems of illegal immigration for so long. Science will always win out.

Alternative Facts #22

The next subject I want to tackle is terrorism. By definition, it is the unlawful use of violence or intimidation to pursue political aims. It is a tactic to get one's way. A powerful tool for bending the will of others to pursue a political point of view. Terrorism creates fear to achieve political, religious, or ideological goals. Historically, it is used against civilians or noncombatants. In the simplest of terms, terrorism exploits human fears to help achieve goals. The term terrorism comes from the French word 'terrorisme' which means to frighten. The usage of the word became popularized in the French Reign of Terror in 1794. Originally, terrorism referred to acts committed by governments in the killing of innocent people. It now has a greater connection with nongovernmental groups. The concept of using terrorism as a tactic to promote a spectacle of fear was advocated by Sergey Nechayev in the early 1900's. It must be noted that terrorism is a tactic and action. It is not a strategy or a game plan. There are some general traits of terrorism that most experts agree upon

1. It is political in its aims and motives.
2. It is violence or there are threats of violence against the public.
3. It has far reaching physical and psychological effects reaching deep into the community and society.
4. Most terrorist acts are committed by one person or a small collective group of individuals. Terrorists disguise their identities and allegiance to blend into the crowd.

Today, when we euphemistically use the term terrorism, we are generally talking about radical Islamic terrorist groups. As with any organization, they have goals. They use the tactic of terrorism to establish precepts to be adhered to by whatever population they govern. Radical Islamic terrorists believe in moral conservatism. They follow the writings of the Koran to the letter and adhere to the Koran's literal interpretation. They attempt to implement Islamic values to all spheres of life in the areas they control. We call this the "advocacy of Islamic fundamentalism." Radical Islam is a monotheistic religious system that prescribes the normative way of life. Radicals, through terrorist tactics, regulate life from cradle to casket. A literal interpretation of the Koran is called *Sunna* by which these radicals practice. Most of the present day radical religious teachings are taught and exposed by *Wahabists* who are part of the Sunni sect of Islam. These religious clerics are ultraconservative.

They preach an intolerant form of Islam. Most of the adherents came from the Saudi Arabian Peninsula. Osama bin Laden and his followers who were responsible for the bombing of the World Trade Center in 2001, followed the beliefs of Wahhabism. They came from Saudi Arabia. ISIL (ISIS), an offshoot led by Abu Bakr Al Baghdadi, follows the general tenants of radical Islam. There are other groups in Africa like Boko Haram and El Shabab that use terrorism as a primary tactic for enslaving their populations. They, as well, follow the tenants of radical Islam.

The abiding relentlessness caused by terrorism is vastly larger than actual casualties. Terrorist acts kill relatively few people but intimidate many. The United States Department of State gathered some statistical information on terrorist attacks for the year 2016.

1. Worldwide there were 11,774 acts of terrorism.

2. The total number of deaths were 28,328.

3. 6,924 of the guests were terrorists themselves.

4. 21,404 casualties were civilian and military.

5. 55% of all attacks were in the following countries; Afghanistan, Bangladesh, Egypt, Iraq, the Philippines, Syria, and Turkey. The total number of deaths in these predominantly Islamic countries were 11,772.

6. The major terrorist groups responsible for the attacks were the Taliban, Islamic state, Boko Haram, El Shabab, the Maoist Communist Party of India, Kurdistan Workers Party and Al Qaeda.

7. 267 casualties from terrorist attacks in Europe.

8. In the United States there were only 68 deaths caused by terrorist attacks in 2016.

9. In totality, more than 12,000 Americans died from gun violence in 2016.

Actual statistics show the number of people killed in the United States in 2016 by terrorists was very small. The death toll of people killed by terrorists was one ten thousand of a percent of our total population.

We have had relatively few attacks, less than 15 in all of 2016. But, one is too many! However, the reality of technology and the access to transportation make zero attacks impossible. Our intelligence agencies, law enforcement departments, and civilians at large have been successful in making the United States one of the safest nations in the Western world. We spend billions of dollars at all levels of government to protect ourselves from terrorist attacks. Most people would say our tax dollars have been spent well. There is little quibbling about the amount. The problem is we cannot build an impermeable wall around our nation for total protection.

We have up to this point been successful in keeping America safe within the restraints of technology. Safety is of paramount importance. There is an overriding political question as to the switch offs between security and our individual freedoms. Should there be government access to our phone conversations? Which Americans should be monitored? Should government have access to our digital footprints? It has been suggested that both conservatives and liberals want the government to have a greater commitment when it comes to protecting the public. That cannot be said of libertarians as voiced by Senators Rand Paul and Ted Cruz. Their first point of advocacy is that civil liberties come first. Most mainstream politicians do not want to hamper or tie the hands of government when it comes to our safety.

For all intent and purposes, most political discussions dealing with terrorism are confined to the Muslim faith. Muslims are people that believe in Islam. Islam is depicted as a religious group that is out of control. They are the poster children of terrorism. In reality, less than 3% of Muslims are radical. 35% to 40% are perceived to be opponents of modernity and Western civilization but are not active participants in terrorism. The remaining majority of Muslims are agnostic when it comes to their religion in reference to other people's beliefs. Radical Islamic attacks in America are rare. It is important we take in account almost all of the attackers on American soil have been home grown. Except for the horrible terrorist act that brought down the World Trade Center in 2001, all acts of aggression by terrorists in the continental United States have been carried out by American citizens that have become radicalized on our shores.

Terrorists have not come onto our nation's soil from foreign countries and perpetrated their hatred upon our population. The actual number of people killed by terrorists in the United States in 2016 was 68. This does not minimize the threat and intimidation poses by terrorism. It puts it in proportion when you realize more than 42,000 Americans were killed by guns in the same year. Terrorism is a threat! There are great political considerations! But, and there is always a but - we must not allow terrorism to breed fear and uncertainty. We must not allow the stress of intimidation and death punish people who believe in Islam. The small number of believers in radical Islam should not be construed as the majority of their faith. There is no evidence that the proposed Trump Muslim Ban on citizens from Syria, Iran, Yemen, Somalia, Sudan, and Libya is necessary. Terrorists have not come on to our shores from any of these countries. Our vetting process for legal immigration is the best in the world. And, there is no evidence illegal immigration is allowing terrorist to cross our borders! We should be forever vigilant. We should even look at ways we can make our vetting process better. However, our desire to keep America safe should not be predicated upon political diatribe or alternative facts. Radical Islam is a threat. It is a threat we must view it as a national priority. In dealing with it, we should not be allowed to dampen our constitutional civil rights.

There are real facts relative to terrorism and immigration. Western Europe has a number of Islamic radical fighters that have come back from Syria and Iraq that have allegiance to ISIL. This is not the case in the United States. There are over 1,500 potential terrorists who have come back from Syria who are now in Europe. In the United States, we have not identified any! This problem must be addressed but we are not Europe. Here, in the United States, our civil liberties do not have to be thrown away to protect ourselves. Political gain and fear mongering in the form of President Trump's Muslim Travel Ban will not make us safer. As stated before, we do not have an impermeable protection against terrorists. The world is not perfect! Our heritage of religious diversity and nation building based upon immigration must be protected. We must safeguard ourselves from radical Islam. But, we must attend to its real impact on our shores. Fear mongering will not lessen the actual damage a terrorist attack will inflict on our nation. Do not buy into the demagoguery of fear. Do not close off our borders. Do not buy into hatred. And, do not vilify other religions and people of color who are painted as potential terrorists.

Alternative Facts #23

Gun control and the Second Amendment is another topic we will address. Gun ownership and any restraints placed upon it are contentious and competing ideas. The culture of guns is deeply rooted into American heritage. There are no clear-cut answers relative to gun controls. Americans feel it is their constitutional right to own guns. But, and there is always a but - how many guns? What kind of guns? With or without any restrictions? Who can own a firearm? Let me present some facts. The ownership of guns and any restraints placed upon them by government are hot political topics. The British Broadcasting Company on January 5, 2016 reported there were 372 mass shootings in the United States in the calendar year 2015. The total number of people killed by firearms on American soil in that year was more than 42,000. This number of firearm deaths was more than 30 times that of the UK. Of all the murders in the United States, 60% came from firearms. Whereas in the United Kingdom, it was less than 10%. There are no official estimates relative to the number of guns in the United States. However, the NRA estimates the number to be more than 300 million. Less than 30% of Americans own a gun. That means the average gun owner owns three guns.

The rights of the public to bear firearms comes from the Second Amendment of the Constitution which states, "A well-regulated militia, being necessary to the security of a free state, the right of the people

to keep and bear arms, shall not be infringed."
We have a long-standing tradition of gun
ownership in our country. There have been
little meaningful restraints to keeping and
bearing arms throughout our 250-year history.
To control firearm ownership is a difficult
charge. Some general facts on guns:

- Firearms are classified into broad categories.
  Handguns, rifles, shotguns, and automatic and
  semi-automatic firearms.

- Handguns represent 55% of all firearms owned
  by the public.

- A 2015 Gallup poll indicates that 60% of all
  guns, mostly handguns, are owned for
  protection against crime. Another 36% of all
  guns are only for the purpose of hunting and
  sports. Finally, 4% are owned for the purposes
  of recreation and target shooting.

- The vast majority of guns are purchased
  legally from gun shops. Another source for the
  purchase of guns comes from gun shows.

    In 2016, there were more than 5,000
major gun shows in the United States. They
represent sales of less than 5% of all guns
purchased. Guns can also be obtained from
private party purchases. This is an unregulated
after market for the sale of guns. It is
impossible to track one person selling to
another. Finally, guns can be purchased in an
illegal market. Estimates are that less than 5%
of all guns are purchased illegally.
Background checks and waiting periods are
involved in the purchase of guns. In most
states there are 'right to carrying' permits that
allow people to carry guns in public.

    Estimates are that one in 20 people
carry concealed weapons upon their person in
public yet only a small fraction have permits

to do so. In 2016, the Pew Research Center stated some general trends on guns and gun ownership.
1. Americans have shown a consistent support for the background checks in the purchases of guns. Two,
2. There should be restrictions on the purchase of guns for the following people. Any individuals on the federal no-fly registry should not be allowed to buy a gun. No guns for the mentally ill. No guns for children.
3. There should be restrictions upon automatic and semi-automatic weapons.
4. The most Americans are in favor of gun ownership with the listed limited restrictions.

There are arguments in favor of gun controls and in opposition to gun controls. The protagonist for gun control argues the following points:
1. The Second Amendment is not an unlimited right for gun ownership.

2. Gun control laws reduce gun deaths.

3. High-capacity magazine should be banned.

4. Gun control laws reduce societal costs associated with crime.

5. The majority of people support background checks and bans on assault weapons.

6. Gun controls lead to fewer suicides.

7. Government-imposed safety features on guns reduces the number of accidental gun deaths.

8. There should be restrictions on gun ownership

because the presence of a gun makes a conflict more lethal.

9. Armed civilian militia are dangerous.

10. Countries with restrictive gun-control laws have lower homicide and suicide rates.

The antagonist for gun controls project the following arguments:

1. The Second Amendment to the Constitution is a total protection for the right to keep and bear arms.

2. Gun control laws do not deter crimes.

3. Gun control laws infringe on the rights of self-defense.

4. Gun control laws directed at limiting automatic weapons infringe upon hunting and sport.

5. Gun control laws will not prevent criminals from obtaining a gun.

6. Gun control laws give too much power to the government.

7. Gun control laws are invasions of privacy.

8. Controls on the right to keep and bear arms are unnecessary. Relatively few people are killed by guns - 12,500 or less a year.

9. Lower gun ownership does not equate to lower suicides.

10. Restricting the sale and ownership of guns would prevent citizens from protecting themselves.

11. Gun control efforts have proven to be ineffective in protecting the public.

A few more concepts relative to gun controls. Amber Phillips in a *Washington Post* article on December 3, 2015, suggested that there are five major questions relative to gun controls. She asked:

1. Would a public holding more firearms present more deaths? Or, is it the other way around?
2. Would more laws relative to gun controls prevent more gun deaths?
3. Should schools' teachers and other educational personnel be allowed to carry guns on campus? Should adult students have the right to carry guns on campus?
4. Is prohibiting gun ownership compatible with the Second Amendment?
5. Do Americans actually want more gun controls?

There are other questions that should be addressed. What gun-control laws currently exist? Will they adequately protect the public if enforced? What has worked to reduce gun violence in other countries? Can we change the culture of guns? Is gun licensing a restriction upon our rights to own a gun?

Alternative Facts #23A

The question of the ownership of guns is an emotional one. It is contentious! There are two sides to it: unfettered ownership of firearms and some type of government regulation upon guns. There are no clear-cut facts that can move a person's emotional stance on the issue of guns. Many Americans are agnostic when it comes to the question of guns. They have never owned one. They have never fired one. And, for some, guns have never been a major consideration in their lives. To other Americans they are essential! They are a defense against the uncertainties of life.

Firearms protect them from personal violations that lurk on the American landscape. Guns are a part of our heritage - the Old West. They defined the individual ruggedness of the American male. In any case, it is evident that guns play a more emotional than factual role in the American psyche. When it comes to guns, facts do not win over emotions! Suffice it to say, the one third of Americans who own guns have control over the gun debate. Organizations like the National Rifle Association have great sway in the political process. It is the very nature of minority rule that allows the gun owner to determine our laws relative to the use of firearms. The National Rifle Association, under the leadership of Peter Brownell and Wayne LaPierre, for all intents and purposes, control the access, purchases, ownership, and the use of firearms in the United States. The NRA is considered the most powerful lobby in the America. Any attempts to put restrictions on the use of firearms is met with the political might of the National Rifle Association and defenders of the Second Amendment.

In other Western nations, particularly Canada and Western Europe, ownership of firearms has been taken out of the hands of the citizenry. From total denial of gun ownership rights to limited usage, primarily for hunting and sport, most other Western nations have strict controls over guns. The vast majority of Americans take this same position. They are in favor of some type of gun control. The general trend in America is the need for the licensing of guns.

Americans support background checks. Americans are opposed to the ownership and sales of semi-automatic and automatic weapons. They are opposed to large magazines that weaponize guns. They are opposed to the sale of lead-based bullets for hunting. Americans want some controls over guns. The overriding question is, what controls and how should they be imposed? There is also the question of time and grandfathering clauses. What type of punishment should be imposed upon people who do not adhere to gun restrictions? There is a definite need for a national debate to determine federal, local, and state laws as applied to firearms. As with any government restrictions, they must be imposed with restraint and education. Nothing draconian! There must be a responsible decision on who has access to guns and what type of guns should be allowed in civil society. Most Americans believe that simple and straightforward gun controls will save lives. Hopefully, restricting guns would bring us to the same measurements of the account that other Western nations have in regard to gun deaths and crimes.

Many people want to interpret the Constitution as being immutable. The National Rifle Association and Second Amendment rights groups feel that the right to bear arms should have no restrictions placed upon it. Their literal interpretation of the Constitution, written in 1789, should hold true today. The NRA refuses to take the dynamics of the last 240 years of our American existence into consideration. They blame any deaths associated with firearms on the people who carry them. They do not accept the fact that having a gun can be causal to deaths and crimes. It is difficult to argue with emotions. It is impossible to tell someone that they should not have the right of gun ownership to protect themselves. If someone breaks into your home or approaches you on the street harboring bad intentions, is having a gun for protection a right? It is hard to argue otherwise! Like any other emotional issue, compromise is difficult. But, and there always is a but - if we restrict the use of automatic weapons in will only effect about 1% of the people who presently own guns. With compromise we can do it in a responsible way. Prohibiting felons, the mentally ill, potential terrorists, and children seems reasonable. Having waiting periods and vetting seems responsible. These ideas are reasonable to a large portion of American citizens, 60% or more. However, the NRA and other Second Amendment groups have the right to impose their will and have done so. Political might is based on will and money. The NRA has both! Their argument is; limited restriction on guns is a slippery slope.

Going down this road will take away the right of gun ownership and the ability for people to protect themselves. In most other countries total gun restriction, at the high end, to small sensible measures to safeguard the public, and at the low end, works. I mentioned U.S. vs. British statistic earlier. They also hold for Canada and Europe. Compromise is important to protect the public and save lives and, hopefully, common sense will prevail and real facts will win over emotions in the debate on gun controls. There is little advocacy for the total banning the ownership of guns in America. Compromise means small changes that will save lives.

Alternative Facts #24

The general notion of taxes is twofold. One, taxes generate revenue for governments. Two, taxes change behaviors of economic players.

There are also two major categories of nongovernmental stakeholders or players in the economy. They are the households and businesses. Taxes alter the production of goods, services and businesses. They can alter consumption and savings pattern in householders or with consumers. Lower taxes point to more production and an expanded GDP. Higher taxes equate to lower levels of economic activity and lower levels of GDP. Taxes are a form of altering one's income stream. Money goes from earners to the government for whatever political purposes are deemed necessary.

There are two major forms of taxes: direct taxes which are levied upon people, such as an income tax and indirect taxes, which are levied upon things, goods and services. An example would be gasoline taxes. When we speak of taxes, there are three types of taxation we refer to:

- Progressive taxes where the higher your income is the greater rate of taxation.
- Regressive taxes with a higher level of income there is a lower the rate of taxation.
- Finally, flat or proportional taxes where all levels of income are taxed at the same rates.

Taxes are used for government services and they affect economic activity. Taxes are levied at the local, state, and federal levels. Let me present a simplified explanation of the Trump tax plan. The Trump administration's tax plan aims to lower taxes for every income earner and business. The goal is to create higher levels of economic activity and standards of living. Economists who adhere to the Trump plan suggest that it will lead to more jobs and economic expansion. They forecast the economy will expand to higher than 96% levels of employment and the GDP will grow at a rate of 3% to 4%. With greater levels of economic activities, government tax revenues will increase. Tax revenues will outpace spending. The federal government's $22 trillion debt will start to dissipate. It is simple supply side economics. But, and there is always a but - the Congressional Budget Office suggests the Trump tax plan will create the polar opposite effect. In the long run, it will lead to a recession and slower levels of economic growth. It will increase the federal debt. The CBO questions the Trump plan's major assumption and forecasts less than 1.5% GDP growth. It forecasts stagflation. False, or alternative facts or assumptions, are at the core of the Trump tax plan. But. there is a silver lining when taxes are lowered! That is, if you are rich. Even if economic activity slows down because of the implementation of the Trump tax reforms the top 1% of income earners will receive a greater share of benefits. Tax savings for people who make more than $250,000 year or more will equate to 90% of all tax savings in the plan. The top 1% of income earners will receive 50% of all tax savings.

A good example of income inequities

caused by Trump's tax reforms is exemplified by an inheritance or death tax. Inheritance taxes at the federal level is at a threshold of $5,450,000. Inheritance taxes can be as high as 45%. If an estate has a value of $5,450,000 or more, the federal government-imposed death tax is 45%. On August 6, 2016, *Money Magazine* initiated a report on a 2015 Congressional Joint Committee on Taxation report. For the fiscal year 2015, a little over 2,600,000 Americans died. Only 4,700 people died during that given year with taxable assets of more than $5,450,000. Only 2/10 of 1% of all estates had to pay inheritance or death taxes. This means that one out of every 500 families had to pay an inheritance tax levied upon the deceased person's assets. This tax is levied only on the very wealthy. The Trump tax plan will eliminate all estate taxes. Effectually, it will only target 1/10 of 1% of all Americans.

Now let us look at general taxpayers proposed tax savings under Trump's plan. I will compare it with the inheritance tax. The United States Census Bureau estimates that in 2016 the average income for a family filing a joint tax return was $56,516. Their tax savings under the new plan would be a little over $1,000. The actual savings to the 4,700 people under the Trump plan would have averaged $2,700,000. There is a large disparity in who saves money. The reasoning is very simple. Under the purposed Trump tax plan, wealthy people will receive greater rates of savings.

This will allow them to invest more. The economy will expand. All segments of the economy will be pulled to higher levels of income. This is the essence of the trickle-down theory. When the average income earner gets a $1,000 tax break, it will not affect their ability to invest. The average income earner does not have enough money to invest. Investment is the purchase of buildings, equipment, and inventories. Investment leads to the outcome is not the general case. Conservatives feel investment is the precipitants of economic activity. The rich who will now have extra dollars to invest because of the Trump tax plan with stimulate more economic activity.

TRUMP TAX PROPOSAL Under this proposal, there are different types of tax savings for both corporate and individual taxpayers.

Alternative Facts #24A

The major tenet of the Trumps tax, plan is, first and foremost, tax savings for the rich. The whole program is predicated upon the trickle-down theory. The backbone of Trump's tax reform is the American Health Act which the Republican Party hopes will replace the American Care Act, better Care known as Obama Care. The AHCA will eliminate the 3.8% surcharge on the top 1% of American income earners. This tax surcharge is meant to subsidize health premiums for the poor. In totality, it is a transfer payment that allowed more than 20 million Americans to have private health insurance. There is another major component to the Trump tax plan. As stated earlier, there will be a complete elimination of the estate tax or, what has been euphemistically called, the death tax. Another change in the tax code will be on the alternative minimum tax. It has limited deductions for the rich. Under the new tax plan, personal income taxes will be affected two-fold.

1. There will be less taxable income brackets.
2. The marginal rate of taxation will be lower.

The proposals of the new tax plan will bring the number of brackets down from 7 to 3 with rate of 10%, 25%, and 35%. Standard deductions will be doubled. The first $24,000 of income will be tax-free. Standard deductions will increase to $12,700 from the existing rate of $6,350. There will be no ceilings on itemized deductions. Tax rates for charitable giving, mortgage interest and retirement savings accounts will remain in place. But, and there is always a but - state and local taxes will not be deductible. The last major change will be capital gains will drop to 20% from the existing 23.8

Winners and Losers

- Winners in the new proposed tax plan will be businesses. Corporate profits will no longer be taxed at 35%. The tax will rate dropped to 15%.

- High income earners will benefit greatly from the new tax plan. The top marginal rate will drop from 39.6% to 35%. There will also be the elimination of the 3.8% tax used to pay for the now abandoned Obama care.

- Tax savings in the form of no estate taxes will benefit the top 1% of net asset valued Americans.

- Creative accounts will continue to extend to hedge fund managers under LLC provisions. They will be taxed at 15%

- The average taxpayer with an income between $56,500 and $75,000 will receive approximately $1,000 a year in tax savings.

- Losers in the new proposal will be upper middle-income earners. There will be an elimination of state and local taxes as a deduction from federal income tax.
- There are no estimates as to the tax proposals impact on the federal deficit.
- 90% of the Trump tax plan savings will go to the top 1% of income earners.

In 2015, the Tax Policy Center estimated that 45.3% of American households, approximately 77,500,000 families, paid no federal tax at all. The remaining 54.7% of earners are paying 100% of the federal taxes. In reality, the top 1% of taxpayers are paying 23% of all taxes. Breaking taxpayers down into tranches of 20%, the lowest 20% pay 0.8% of all federal income tax. The next tranche, or the second lowest 20%, pay 3.4%. Median income earners are effectively paying 9.2% of all taxes. The second highest tranche is paying 17.5% of all taxes. And, the wealthiest 20% of Americans are paying 69% of all federal income taxes. This analysis from the Tax Policy Center for 2015 is generally acceptable to all tax experts. The tax cuts proposed by the Trump plan are cutting taxes for the rich by a greater percentage than tax cuts for the average middle income American. This tax proposal is regressive in nature. If in fact the trickle-down theory works, the Trump tax plan will make America great again. But, there is no statistical proof that lower levels of income or corporate taxes create a large enough economic stimulation to expand or enhance the middle class. The contrary is true.

During the Eisenhower administration, marginal tax rates were exceedingly high and the middle class expanded. During the Kennedy/Johnson administrations, marginal tax rates were lowered with increases in income for the middle class but at a lower rate of growth than the top 20% tranche. Looking at the Nixon, Carter, Ford, Reagan, and Bush administrations, lowering the taxes for the wealthy did not equate to greater standards of living for the middle-class. The greatest gains in middle-class standards of living took place during the Clinton administration where marginal rates of taxation were almost constant. Trump's tax plans are no more than a redistribution of wealth from the middle and poor to the rich. The fact of the matter is the trickle-down theory or supply side economics does not work. Accepting alternative facts or truths is what has brought about a decreasing or leveling out of middle-class incomes for the last 30 years. The United States has seen a shrinking middle class for over three decades. During this same period of time, the wealthy have accumulated greater rates of income and assets. From the year 2000 to the present, the United States has the worst distribution of wealth in its last 100 years of our history. Much of the shrinkage of the middle class is attributed to the trickle-down theory and tax policies of the federal government.

An author's note: most Americans do not know much about taxes other than they exist and that they are too high. With almost ½ of income earners not making enough money to effectively pay income taxes, people have little first-hand knowledge about taxes. The vast majority of taxes that the average American pays are at the local or state level. These taxes are in totality regressive. They are collected when consumer transactions take place. They are thoughtless and painless because the tax in included into the sales price of goods and services. There are some laws of taxation.

1. People must have the ability to pay them.
2. There must be a certainty and consistency

about paying them.

3. They must be easy to collect.

4. Taxes cannot be at the expensive of investment. These rules were developed by Adam Smith in his book, <u>Wealth of Nations</u> in 1776.

They still hold today. People only understand taxes when they make enough money to pay them out of their pockets. When your income gets high enough that you pay estimated taxes, you understand them. When you have an escrow account for tax payment attached to some kind of debt instrument, you understand them. Taxes are an emotional and fiscal burden. As you earn more, tax consequences on your earnings might be of greater import than earnings themselves. Most Americans never reach this level of income. We need a tax policy that directs high earners to spend or invest their monies that promotes economic expansion and income equity. This is simple!

Give tax breaks for investment, the purchase of building, equipment, and inventories. Not for speculation. If someone invests and creates new goods and services which expands employment, they should pay less tax. Speculation is just trading already produced goods or services. It creates nothing more than paper profits. It promotes the inequity of wealth!

Let me give you an example of this notion of investment verses speculation. When IPO's- Initial Public Offerings-are purchased, the money from investors go to the company or corporation to produce goods and services. There is economic expansion. Jobs are created and, therefore, these investments should be taxed at a low rate. When people trade existing stocks or flip houses, in effect paper is traded. No money goes to the company or corporation to cause economic expansion or jobs.

Speculation should be taxed at a much higher rate than investment. Lower taxes on investment and greater taxes on speculation is a tax policy. This type of tax policy could be a pseudo trickle-down theory with government direction. It will benefit the middle and poor and will not dampen the incentives of the rich to invest their monies.

This is one of many examples of how we can use tax policy to make America great again. Do not buy into giving the rich more with they hope something will trickle down to you. Crumbs are not enough. The last 30 years have proven that.

Alternative Facts #25

Principled people are different than those who are ideologically driven. People with principles live in the world of facts. Using a rigorous approach of filtering out fact from fiction, they come up with scientifically derived conclusions. Ideological people only sift through information to validate their beliefs. To them, facts are not important. In most circumstances, evidence-based conclusions are abandoned in favor of conformity to their beliefs or faith. Anything that supports ideology is acceptable. The ends always legitimize their goals. Ideologist are willing to throw away the truth in order to legitimize their beliefs. Anything, no matter how unreasonable or illegitimate, is acceptable if it falls into the schema of their existence.

Now let us look at another hot topic. The differences in conservative ideology and progressive principles are crystal clear when it comes to Social Security. Conservatives want to privatize it! They want to create individual investment type platforms for each and every individual. All decisions with private investment accounts should be made by the individuals who pony up their money. Instruments like IRA accounts, 401(k) accounts, tax-sheltered annuities, investments in stocks, bonds, and real estate are individual type investments. They should not be under the umbrella of government decision making. There should be no government guarantees as to the rate of return on these individual investments. Their return on their contributions should be market-driven. The accounts should be for that individual and only that individual. A progressive or liberal position on Social Security is different. Social Security is an insurance policy! It is not a personal investment. The contributors or people who pay into Social Security pay for claims made by others in the insurance pool. Contributions are not for one's own retirement or pension accounts - they are for other people in the pool. Actuarially claims are spread over a great number of people to lower risk.

The Social Security act of 1935 began as a major tool to combat unemployment during the Great Depression. It is the antecedent to today's Social Security Administration. The program was part of the New Deal package developed by Franklin Delano Roosevelt. It was a counter to the rigors of the economic downturn in the late 1920's and early 1930's. The first Social Security payment was made in 1937. Benefits were lump sum payments to the families of deceased workers. The first monthly payments for the retired were issued on January 31, 1940. Today, there are more than 65 million people collecting benefits. To show you how Social Security has grown since 1935, there were less than 60,000 beneficiaries in its first year, 1937. Since then there has been an expansion and escalation of the basic program.

The idea behind Social Security was simple. People who were working would pay a payroll tax to fund a retiree's pension. They would pay for someone who had worked in the past and had contributed to the United States economy and the American way of life. The rational for Social Security is much like the rational for helping out our arm services. Our military has protected American from outside threats. Many service people have given up their lives. They have lost arm and limb. They have sacrificed years of their lives and income to safe guard our way of life. For their protection, we make their future safer and more comfortable. We transfer our treasure to them for their sacrifices. It is a transfer payment. It is their right. It is part of the American way of life to receive a thank you for what they have done for us. Social Security is much the same. We take care of our own workers in their later years because it is the right thing to do. Retired American workers have the right, the guarantee, to be protected in their senior years for what they did for us. They have laid down the foundations for our opportunities to be safe and prosperous.

At its inception, for every person who collected Social Security benefits, there were 42 people who were taxed at a rate of 1.5% of their income. The first generation of recipients would be funded by a much larger second-generation pool of workers. This was matched by employers to create a fund of monies for recipients. As the population grew, the second generation would be funded by an even larger third generation. The costs of the taxes would in effect grow smaller as the population grew younger by people having more children. America's population was forecasted to grow larger and younger. When a person retired and received Social Security, his benefit package would be approximately 10% of his earnings. It was considered to be a partial retirement program. Hopefully, it would be augmented by an individual's investments or savings. With the advent of changing demographics, less population growth than forecasted and people getting older because of medical advances, the program's costs have mushroomed. To add to the cost of Social Security, other groups were included into Social Security rolls. People are now eligible for benefits if they are members of the worker's family, children and spouses. There are benefits for dependent children up to the age of 18. There is money for spouses who have never worked or made payments into the system. Medicaid and Medicare were added to Social Security in 1965 by President Lyndon B. Johnson. Supplemental security income (SSI) was added in the early 1970's. It gave benefits to the disabled and elderly regardless of their work history.

Demographic variables and an array of new claimants have made Social Security a large social expense. It is a run-away transfer payment to conservatives and the cost of being an American to the progressives. Conservatives view it as a privilege that is costly and can be taken away. Progressive view it as a right that is guaranteed. Conservatives view it as a private product. Liberals view it as a public good. Let us look at its history. The first recipient who collected the first checks in the late 1930's did not receive a payment until he was 62 years old. Initially over 95% of recipients were men. Women did not get into the employment ranks until World War II. Today there are more women in the work force than men. Demographics have changed. Statistically the first people who receive claims lived until they were 63 years old. Social Security payments lasted for a little bit more than 11 months after retirement. People died at a much younger age than today. Today's recipients can still receive Social Security payments at 62. These are partial payments. Full payment starts at 66. People who receive Social Security on average live until the early 80's. The average recipient receives money for more 150 payments meaning they are paid benefits for more than 14 years. That was not the case in 1937. Total Social Security payments and benefits today are almost 35% of a person's income as opposed to 10% in 1937. The program is vast and expanding. The Congressional Budget Office has forecasted that the Social Security fund will run out of money in the next 25 years. Something has to be done.

Here is where the difference between conservatives and liberals is most pronounced. For the Social Security fund to be viable in the future there must be higher tax rates. There must be lower benefits. People might have to wait until they are older to receive benefits. Social Security taxes max out at $118,000 at a tax rate of 7%. This cap must be raised. All of these variables have to change even if you are progressive. There is one basic truth - Social Security is not sustainable the way it is today. Conservatives want to privatize it and, if it is privatized it becomes an individual's investment. It is not a societal problem. It is a personal problem. Conservatives feel a person's failure or success is no one business but their own. Retirement is not a government responsibility. Progressives feel if Social Security is a public good, then we all have a stake in it. The questions are:

- Who pays for it?

- How much does it cost?
- What are the rightful claims?
- Should it be paid for through progressive or regressive taxes?

If Social Security is viewed as an investment, which is the case in the conservative community, then the rate of return is exceedingly low. It is less than 2%. Therefore, conservatives want to privatize Social Security which would hopefully increase its rate of return to more than 5%. Progressives or liberals feel Social Security is an insurance policy. The transfer of monies from the younger population to the older population is not at the direction of the marketplace. If the returns on the invested Social Security fund are too low, claims by beneficiaries must be subsidized by the government. Two distinctly different philosophies. One is individual privatization of investments for the claimant's future incomes which is market driven and has market risk. The other is an insurance policy which the government directs and subsidizes.

Alternative Facts #25A

Authors note: when we talk about transfer payments, welfare, there are always winners and losers. The people who pay taxes forgo income. Many taxpayers view themselves as losers. Their money is going to someone they may feel are unworthy. Tax revenues can come from many sources. In totality, taxes can be either regressive, proportional, or progressives. In any case, taxpayers fund welfare programs. Recipients may feel like losers as well. Monies that go into the programs that are set up to help the poor may have restrictions. In some cases, the programs are not always helpful. Sometimes the monies are locked up in bureaucratic situations that exacerbate the hardships of the poor. For the payers, the rich, and for the receivers, the poor. They both lose the freedom of choice. The government is supposed to act as an intermediary between the payers and the recipients. This process historically has been clumsy and inefficient. Decisions are taken out of the individuals' hands and put into the hands of a government bureaucrat. It is clear to both conservatives and progressives that this process is lacking.

In the best of circumstances, transfer payments come from people who can afford to give up part of their income stream. Hopefully, tax dollars are taken from people where it does not interfere with either their normal consumption or investment habits. These monies are held to be meager or a small pittance to the wealthy people. However, they are substantial to the poor recipient. Small sums of money from the rich are like golden nuggets to the poor. If the monies are used properly, they can create transformative situation for the disadvantage. The government acts as an intermediary to lineup money for the needs of the poor. It should be a process where everyone is satisfied, both rich and poor. There should be equity for both the payer and recipient. We must make note of the bureaucratic inefficiency between the taxpayer and the recipient. Bureaucracies have a way of muddying up the waters.

Once welfare programs are started they are rarely taken away. In most cases, transfer payments are Band-Aids. They do not create a situation where the recipient can better his or her skills to be competitive in the marketplace. The intent of helping people through transfer payments in many cases is hijacked by the bureaucracy. We have all been victims of public inefficiency. We all feel bureaucratic arrogance, their heartlessness in dealing with us, and their lack of empathy. Go to any government office and it becomes apparent that something is amuck.

People die if there is no safety net. Social Security is the lifeline for millions of retired Americans. People die when goods and services are not delivered due to bureaucratic inefficiency. They die if there are no programs to sustain the poor in economic hard times. Seniors die if there are no provisions for their later years. Not every American is successful enough to provide for themselves in hard times. There is a public need for government aid. We also have a problem as who to tax. We must tax the right people for the right amount of money to deal with social problems. Politics and falsehoods can get into the way of transfer payments as a means to help the disadvantage.

There is another problem. On the other side of the ledger, there is welfare fraud. 10% to 12% of all recipients are receiving benefits they are not entitled to. People are taking advantage of welfare programs through fraud and deceit. They lie, they cheat, and steal to get something for nothing. Welfare is complicated enough. We do not need cheaters. There is also the question of who should pay for Social Security or any other welfare program?

- How much should they pay?
- How long should welfare programs be in place?
- Since money is not free, what are the opportunity costs of welfare projects?
- What else could be done with the money?

Again, let us look at the recipient. In urban areas, they are nonwhites. In rural areas the vast majority are white. In both cases, welfare recipients are generally uneducated. There are viewed as freeloaders and lazy.

These characteristics are not always true, but the taxpayer feels their monies are going for an unworthy cause. The poor recipient has little political clout. These factors present an image of Social Security recipients as social liabilities. They should be viewed as a treasured asset. The elderly helped create our heritage. They opened up opportunities to allow a new generation of Americans to prosper. The issue of Social Security is emotional on both sides, the taxpayers and the recipients. Payroll taxes are a financial burden to the people who pay them. These taxes create a negative feeling towards the recipient. To the recipient monies contributed by others are a lifeline. Transfer payments are a necessity. They are a social imperative. Without Social Security elderly people could die.

Social Security is complex, nuanced and difficult. But, and there is always a but -. if we do not help the elderly and the poor what will become of them? We said on an earlier occasion the marketplace is such that if one cannot fend for his or herself then they should look to their family for help. If the family cannot help, they should look to the church. If God does not want them, then the government is the family of last resort. People who believe in Social Security and other welfare programs view it as part of the social contract. If you cannot help yourself, if your family cannot help you, if the church does not have enough resources to help you, then we look to the government. The burden of poverty can be lessened by transferring wealth from those who have it to those who are in need. Capitalism has many great qualities. There is no greater productive engine for wealth. But, and there is always a but - capitalism creates income inequities. Charity is a solution. Philanthropy is a primary quality of a great nation.

Should the individual's charity fill the wealth void for millions of Americans? Should the government mandate transfer payments to fill the void? These are basic questions. Capitalism is the ultimate engine to build wealth and high standard of living. However, there are certain things that the marketplace cannot bring to the table. It cannot feed, nor house, nor medically take care of its people.

These tasks are in the realm of government if you are progressive. The tools government use are blunt and sometimes inefficient. But, these transfer payments are needed. They ameliorate societal problems caused by a bad distribution of wealth which is an unintentional consequence of capitalism. Conservatives think the needs of people who are not successful can be met by charity. The people who are at the margins need the aid from the people who are at the top. If we do not help the poor through programs like Social Security and charity, people will die. Social Security and other major welfare programs are predicated upon taxing those who can afford to help those in need. Even in the 1880's in Bismarck's Germany, they felt the need for social programs.

Most Western nations had established Social Security programs before the United States. In all European countries it is a right, not a privilege, to be taken care of. Do not let alternative facts cause you to turn a blind eye to the subject. Social Security is an insurance program to help the elderly and sick. It is not an investment instrument. Not all Americans have the financial ability to pay for themselves. They have lived on the margins their whole lives. They never had the ability to save for their future needs. Progressives feel it is better to tax the rich who have made the most of their opportunities. We tax the people who can most afford to be charitable. Progressive socialize charity in the form of social programs. They take from the rich to help the poor. A case can be made that not only treasure, but choice, is taken from the tax-payer. The fact of the matter is Social

Security is expensive. It is a draw on
investment. It takes away personal choice. It
is all of the above. But, in a compassionate
nation, it is right thing to do.

Alternative Facts Epilogue

I can talk about alternative facts ad nauseam. Falsehoods are out there to bolster both the conservative and progressive agendas. I could have been more scholarly. For some of you, I should not have been so bias. But, and there is always a but - we need to respect real facts. Lies, big and small, roll off our tongues too easily. They are harmful! The worst part about prevarication is that lies are so freely acceptable. We must face the fundamental question of why do we accept falsehoods? Why do we accept cheap truths to live by when they are so hurtful to the people who need the most help? Why do we accept lies that bifurcate our world into a few who have so much and the many who have so little?

If I have done anything in offering up this book, it would be to bring about intellectual curiosity and recognition that something is wrong with our political process. We should recognize that we must fight the good fight for others even if it means doing it at our own expense. We must be mindful that we live a hurried leisure life at the expense of making rational decisions predicated upon facts. We must be aware that on a societal and on an individual basis we have to sacrifice for others as well as ourselves. We should be inclusive not exclusive.

Hopefully, I have championed the thought that we should have done better. We cannot let alternative truths be the bases for decision- making. We cannot let lies destroy everything we hold dear. On a personal note, I was at a round table discussion on trade a while ago. The moderator finished the program by saying:

I have a few ideas I would like to pass along to all of you. If you leave this program and are irritated, we did a good job." Irritation and stretching the boundaries of intellectual comfort bring about truth and change. I know you have heard points of view that are antithetical to your personal views. This is good my friends! If you leave here and say that S.O.B. was not evenhanded, that is good. He was biased. He was not truthful. And, if you decided to look into what I have said, then I have done a good job! If you are irritated at the conservative or progressive contributors to our round table to such an extent that you will look into the veracity of what they have said, they have also have done a good job. On your way home, if you ponder on what you have heard we accomplished much my friends. This round table is only important if it opened your eyes. If it created intellectual curiosity and has forced you to be more open to a different position. We may have reinforced your ideas or brought about a fundamental change in your thinking. Both are equally important. I ask no more of you than be open-minded and curious. Grapple for a more truthful way of looking at the fundamental problems that plague our social and political arenas. Earlier I said truth cannot hurt us as individuals or collectively as a society. Truth is the antiseptic or the cleanser that casts a brighter light upon the acceptable. As you leave this room, I ask you to push for the pursuit of truth. A new clarity that is fact based can only make our existence better.

Before we leave, I want to present one final example of what I consider to be a reprehensible misrepresentation of the truth. The Trump administration's EPA is denying a 2017 climate report from the National Academy of Sciences. The Academy, in collaboration with several federal agencies, proclaimed that climate change is real. It poses an eminent danger to our way of life. The report simply states a fact. An irrefutable truth. Increases in greenhouse gases caused by human activity have made the Earth's temperature rise. The EPA, as well as the Department of Energy, have been suppressing data and research on global warming. They have directed all of their employees as of August 8, 2017, to no longer use the phrase climate change – it has been changed to "weather extremes." Employees must use the phrase "increase nutrient efficiency" from this point on instead of "greenhouse gas accumulation." This a clear, insidious way of misrepresenting the truth. A simple subterfuge and a falsehood of epic proportion. It is an overreach to help the fossil fuel industry, the coal industry, and a conservative right wing of the Republican Party. All of this obviously at the expense of humanity. Global warming is a fact! Hundreds of thousands of people worldwide will suffer immeasurable harm, even death, from the ravages of global warming. To deny its existence or intentionally understate its importance, is not only reprehensible, it is immoral. In Al Gore's new book, <u>An Inconvenient Sequel: Truth to Power</u>, written in 2017, he exemplifies the problem of global warming as a ticking clock. Ecological problems if left unaddressed will break up the very bedrock of our existence. Let us not forget that the damage human beings do to the Earth can be irreparable. What we do today will affect future generations. The unintended consequence of our selfishness can condemn future generations to great hardship, even death. We need to view our actions in a rational way. Facts and science, not faith in the unknown or lies, are the only paths that can confront the vicissitudes of our existence. Truth will give us the best chance of a future that can hold an understanding of the best that we can be. We must be mindful that the collective is more important than the individual. "Only accepting truth, not alternative facts, will lead us to a brighter future" were the moderator's, D.W. Martin's last words.

Once he was done, he paused and walked out of the room. I shall do the same.